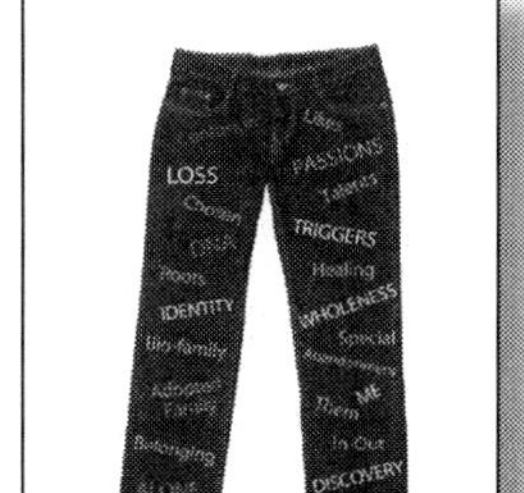

Pulling on New Genes:

WOUNDS-TRIGGERS + HEALINGS:
An Adoptee's Journey Through Life

This story is told from the perspective of an adoptee who, as a birthmother, relinquished her child and who is now in loving reunion and works as a spirit healer.

Liz Ashling, Doctorate, CHT

Pulling on New Genes: Wounds-Triggers + Healings: An adoptee's Journey through Life
Liz Ashling

Copyright 2012

Cover design by Liz Ashling and Teresa Southwell

Spirit Journey Publishing
PO Box1214
Bernalillo, NM 87004
E-mail: Ashlingbook@comcast.net

If you are unable to order this book from your local bookseller, you may order directly from the publisher by contacting her using her email address above.

Library of Congress Cataloging-in-Publication Data.
Ashling, Liz

Summary: An adoptee's journey through life. A book of healing and spiritual awakening told from the perspective of an adoptee who, as a birthmother, relinquished her child and who practices as a spiritual healer.

ISBN 978-0-578-13082-8, printed on acid–free paper in the United States.

Dedicated to my Adopted Mom and Dad, who always stood by me even when I was not aware.

To all my friends and the many healers on my path who continued to support me when I was blind to my journey and assisted in opening my eyes to new directions.

To Allison, who was the first to encourage and assist me in my writing, and to Jane, who read my work and knew its value and encouraged my new voice, acknowledging my writing and its need for the adoption community.

To the Dave Thomas Foundation, which acknowledges adoption as a lifelong journey which told me it was time to complete my book.

To Kay and Janet for the book cover ideas and to Teresa for bringing the cover into reality.

To my editor, Inkslinger Editing, who prepared my book for publishing, and to Cody, who picked up my project at the last hour and produced the final book design.

I thank my sisters for holding their views so I could find my own.

To my daughter for wanting to find me and, in doing so, healing and giving me family in a whole new way.

To my partner Sheri, who helps keep me grounded each day.

To my soul, who whispered to me for twenty years to keep writing.

Table of Contents

Within these chapters people's names have been changed to honor their privacy.

This is not a victim story, but stories of coming home to one's true self. Within this book are stories that illustrate ways to reclaim life without historical roots, or one's biological mother and father and their special vibrations to guide you. Throughout my life I have learned how to move from my wounded self into wholeness by facing the void, loneliness, and my fears of abandonment. This story details the complexity of being adopted and explains the dual stories that get created from not knowing your roots. It is a story of coming back into balance through searching for heart/ passion, uniqueness, and life gifts.

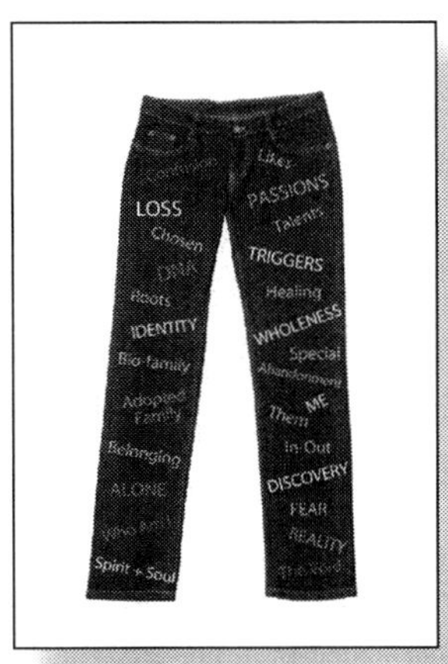

Foreword to a Journey in Healing the Abandonment Wound the Void

I believe every life path is a spiritual journey chosen by our soul for our own spiritual growth. Adoption is no different in this regard. Indeed, adoption is a gift for many. It brings together children in need with parents in need, creating connections where connection might not otherwise exist.

Within my own adoptive family, I knew I was loved and I was told I was special. But within this framework, I also was expected to like and do what my family's interests were. In this grew a tension that is the narrative of this book—and the healing of this tension is the book's heart. Essentially, in order to do what my family liked, I believed I had to give up what I liked and who I truly was. My family's choices were different from what I valued and wanted for my life, so overtime these differences and inconsistencies caused me to distance myself from my family. The pain of this emotional separation caused me to look inward to discover for myself who I am. Years into my development I see these many wounds as my greatest gifts.

As with anything, there are both easy adoptions and difficult ones, loving supportive families and families of confusion and denial. My story is not told to diminish or exalt the adoption experience. It is told with the hope that the truth of the adoptive process and the experience for everyone involved be acknowledged and honored in order to mend the wounding inherent in separating any child from his or her birth parents. And as good as adoption is, the child often enough does incur major wounds. And, as good as adoption is, pretending that these wounds don't exist is ultimately more wounding. It teaches the child not to recognize the truth of his or her own feelings.

It is my hope in sharing this story that the lessons specific to the life experience of adoption are illuminated in a way that promotes healing and well-being for those on this path. I also wish to bring greater awareness to the issues and concerns of the birth parents, the adoptees, and the adoptive parents—issues that may have been overlooked or ignored traditionally, leading to a higher percentage of certain dysfunctional behaviors or choices among adoptees, thus lowering their quality of life and diminishing their capacity for achieving balance, well-being, and wholeness in life.

With this in mind, it is my desire that those individuals who are adopted might find insightful ways through my story to face possible feelings of abandonment and loneliness and to stop creating isolation and other destructive behaviors. It is my intention to provide new avenues for people to awaken to their authentic self and to create their life from their core. I also hope that in capturing my internal struggles on paper, I might provide a way for others to walk in my shoes. This book also can serve as a learning vehicle for adoptive parents, social workers and therapists that work in the adoption field. It might provide a greater understanding of what goes on within adoptees, allowing these parents a way of assisting these children in finding their wholeness and their life gifts, a way home to themselves.

I feel I must begin with something challenging to think about. Without her or his birthmother, an adoptee can be left searching for ways to fill a vibrational void (the missing mother's heart beat) and for the keys to who they are. The void is created when we are separated from our birthmother without adequate bonding time. The void grows ever deeper, then, when we are separated from any knowledge of our own DNA, from knowing our roots or our family history. It is not from the lack of love from our new family. Without knowing our own DNA, our family roots or the continuation of feeling our birthmother's heartbeat, we are driven to search for something more, something to fill this void or hole we feel in our hearts.

There is an assumption that a family can adopt a child and give them their family history—assimilate them into the family, so to speak. My adoptive family is the only family I know, but their family origin and DNA history are unique to them. I share their history because I was raised and socialized with them. I have shared in their history, culture and customs—but in my DNA, I am me, and I have my own history and cultural imprinting in my blood and cell memory. "The wisdom of all human ancestors and their lessons are coded in the DNA of the blood" (Jamie Sams, author of the book 13 Clan Women). It is time to understand this knowledge and to act by providing avenues for adopted children to find their own wholeness so that they can connect to their larger story.

Expecting the child to be like them, the adoptive parents can create misconceptions that disconnect adoptees further from their DNA and from a deep knowing of themselves. We need to recognize the child's DNA history and give them as much information as possible—otherwise the child can lose his or her true identity. Providing truthful information about their history can assist them in discovering themselves. Acknowledging their losses can help bridge the gap created out of the confusion of living out of two separate stories: the first being "I was abandoned" and the second being "I am chosen." Without known roots, the adoptee is left to swing between these two realities. She or he acts and acts out accordingly.

The lack of knowing one's DNA can be a metaphor to describe the deep and profound emotional, spiritual, physical and psychological connection to the self. Without DNA–knowing, the adoptee is haunted by this void, particularly when forming individual identity. But this is also a legal issue—over half the states still have closed adoption records unless the adoption is an open adoption. Adoptees deserve the same starting place as all children—simply the knowing of their roots and family history.

From my perspective, what is missing from the adoptee's life can be filled in through three important things. **First, awareness**—telling the truth. **Second, consciousness**—being awake and committed to the adoptee's needs. And **three, love.** These come from the adoptee themselves, but they also come from the adoptee's family and circle of support. Helping an adoptee find his or her true life gifts and passions, the things that truly bring them joy, can lead an adoptee into his or her heart wisdom. Acknowledging and discussing the child's feelings of loss and separation of the adoptee's birth family assists in healing the abandonment wound. Knowing what creates joy assists to heal the heart wound of abandonment. Understanding the profound wound of abandonment is the soul journey of an adoptee. It is a difficult journey, but it can also be a beautiful one.

PULLING ON NEW GENES, then, is not a victim narrative, but one of coming home to one's true self. Within are stories that illustrate ways to reclaim life without historical roots and without one's biological mother and father or their special vibrations to guide you. Throughout my life I have learned how to move from my wounded self into wholeness by facing the void, loneliness, and my fears of abandonment. PULLING ON NEW GENES details the complexity of being adopted and explains the dual stories that get created from not knowing your roots.

It is a story of coming back into balance by searching for heart/passion, uniqueness, and life gifts.

All of us experience pain, and our strengths and gifts come from walking into and through it. In action we face our demons and learn our life lessons. The pain is our whetstone, our edge in finding our true selves. I am happy to report today I have finally learned to stand true to myself. When I feel loss—whether from the death of a loved one to the ending of an intimate relationship—I can stay present and no longer abandon myself.

PART ONE:

The Abandonment Wound — Loss — Adoption Confusion

Chapter One: The Beginning—The Primal Wound

As a soul I come from universal oneness, filled with love and light. My time has come to voyage to the earth plane for the next leg of my journey. I'm ready; I've chosen this Earth journey. I leave my disembodied state and enter the fetus within the womb of my new mother. I feel the density of my body, small and compact, not totally formed. I play with these boundaries moving fully into my earth form. I sense my body's warmth as I float, swaying gently with her movements within the warm fluid of my mother's belly. It feels different here in this container, but I can feel love here.

I settle in deeper. I am aware of everything around my mother and me. I can hear the sounds of sweet music playing and bits of conversations. I'm aware of my mom's emotions, joy, love, uncertainty, and warmth. I'm even sensitive to other people around my mom. I notice a tube running from my belly to hers; it feeds and nurtures me. I feel secure. I take in her nourishment, I sleep and I grow. I'm lulled by her heartbeat, this particular rhythm belonging to her. I am growing into a human child soon to be birthed here on earth. I float in the warmth around me, I grow, I'm nurtured, and my heart beats in the rhythm of my mom. It feels so good hearing the thud, thud, thud, thud of each heartbeat; it is comforting somehow. Her rhythm defines me. I'm merged with her.

As time passes I begin to feel a little uneasy. I'm receiving lots of weird feelings, and some of them have put me on guard. I feel disconnected from love, yet I'm still here in my warm home in my mom's belly. I can hear my mom's thoughts and feel her fears. I pickup her contradictory messages and it rattles my cells. I feel love all around me mixed with warnings.

"I have to give you away. I can't keep you. How did this happen to me anyway?"

My body registers the shock of these statements along with times of withdrawal. I wonder when this warmth will disappear? I brace myself for an unknown future. At times I am surrounded by sadness and love, these feelings of big waves wash over my tiny frame. These feelings enter me through my umbilical cord with my food; I have absolutely no control over it. While I grow in the womb I take in all the contradictory messages. They unsettle. Some days I feel bright, and other days I feel sad and lost. I feel the enormous loss to come.

My birth time is near; I chose to imagine love outside of the womb. I wonder what air will be like. How will I be greeted outside of my mother's womb? What will the next phase of life be like? It's time, I push out through the birth channel into the earth world filled with air … and new sounds, I breathe my first breath, and then I'm greeted by well-meaning strangers. They take me away from my mother and her familiar rhythm. I don't know it then, but I will never feel her heartbeat or her unique rhythm again.

A big woman with large soft hands washes me tenderly and wraps me in a soft, warm, light green blanket. She smells foreign. She carries me gently into a large room filled with cribs, each containing a tiny newborn baby. She finds an empty crib and places me into it. Then she leaves. My mother is nowhere near, nothing is familiar; I am alone. I am conscious of my own rhythm but it seems empty without my mom's heartbeat. I long for the safe, warm feelings of my mom. Different people come and go, they feed and wash me, some hold me, my physical needs are taken care of, but the nurturing safe rhythm of my mother is gone. I lie in my crib in terror and alone. I long for the comfort and safety of the womb, I long for the rhythm and heartbeat I've known for the past nine months, I long for the smell and the touch of my mother. Where is she, the one who gave me life?

I spend endless days in the hospital, different people caring for me. There seems to be a routine of food, holding, bathing, holding, sleep. Then one day a man and woman come to see me. They smile and are gentle. They pick me up and wrap me in a new blanket and carry me away, out of the nursery, down a long hallway and out of the hospital. Their energy of love and excitement surround me. I want to fall into their love, their touch. They tell me they are taking me home to live with them and they are very happy. I'm happy but their vibration is so different, they seem foreign to me. I feel contentment and unsettled at the same time. Inside I'm crying, "I want my mother. I want to feel her love. Where is she?" Although I feel the love of my new parents, I still long for the love and familiar vibration of my mother, I long for the familiar sound of her heartbeat—and will throughout my life.

The great heart wound has been set in place—the abandonment of my mother is complete—and I begin my life here on the earth plane with these wounds and with a new set of parents who love me.

This is my beginning, as an infant to be adopted.

Note to my reader: Healing the loss of the child's birth mother's heartbeat, the primal wound, the void, can be found in exercises in Part Four: Healing Exercises.

Chapter Two: Where Did I Come From?

When I was four years old, I was told I was adopted, chosen and loved. The only information told to me at the time was that my birth mom and dad had two boys a few years older than me, and that my dad was called away to war and was killed before I was born. My mom was poor and felt she couldn't take care of me, so she put me up for adoption.

As a youngster these stories registered as an unconscious conflict between feeling abandoned and feeling fortunate to being chosen by my adopted family. My body and unconscious mind registered this duality at a deep cellular level, holding this information for me to consider and confront throughout my life. Although I was abandoned at birth, I carried the conscious story that I was chosen and special into my life. I felt fortunate to be part of my family and to have loving parents to care for me. The abandoned child was rescued and safe. As I grew I felt grateful and I was respectful, because always lurking in the back of my mind was the realization that I could be in an orphanage without a family or a place to call home.

Feelings of inclusion and safety can be difficult to manage as a child, and these were exacerbated in my case by the quick changes to come in our family. Within seven months of my arrival, my mother became pregnant. Soon, a younger sister was born, followed by two additional children, another sister and a brother. The arrival of my younger sister likely complicated my bonding process with my mom. Her attention was pulled away from me and directed toward the new life growing within her womb. Since I spent the first three months in a hospital, it was crucial that we have extra bonding time to stabilize and ground me physically and emotionally. I needed more time to feel connected and to create a sense of belonging—I needed her heartbeat and the security that she was truly there for me. Mom's pregnancy took her energy away from building this strong relationship, and therefore I was left without naturally forming a solid connection. My adopted mom's subtle withdrawal accentuated my deeper feelings of being outside, alone, and disconnected. This was not conscious, of course. On the outside everything seemed fine. I was still the new arrival to the family, greeted with the joy and pride of any newborn.

But the inner child wants to be held for hours, to be petted and stroked and pampered and loved as a newborn. My inner child wants to be seen, have her fingers and toes counted, and validated that she is complete and perfect just the way she is. She wants to be admired and told how beautiful she is and how glad you are she was born. She wants to be important to you, to count, to feel she belongs no matter what. She wants to be liked. Underneath everything she wants is to know she is loved and secure.

Over the years I did many things to get these needs met. I had sex with people in order to be held, stroked and pampered. I withheld my truth and gave in to other people's ideas to fit in and not feel alone. I learned when it was safe to tell my truth. In large family gatherings where I felt unheard, I was silent and polite. I tried to be my best at everything; I have extremely high standards for myself and the other people in my life. I tried to look great all the time so that I would be admired and seen as beautiful. My outside image became extremely important. I tried things I didn't want to do to belong. One birthday when my date was two hours late, I not only felt abandoned, I felt I wasn't really here. Unhealed, the mind distorts the inner child's needs.

I grew up in a large gray stucco house, filled with love, opportunity and family ritual, a member of a large family yet without a sense of belonging. We lived in the same neighborhood until my parents retired. I was popular with my friends, adventurous, and cool. I felt part of the community, yet disconnected and not knowing the reasons for these feelings. I shook them off until one day my shadow grew so large it ate me, and I had to wake up and face the sad, lost, fearful parts of myself that ran me. I had to stop and go into the sadness and discover my core wounds— the wounds of disconnection and the wounds from not knowing my birth family origins. I had to stop and heal the loss of my birth mother and birthfather and honor the abandoned feelings that ran me. I had to learn how to recreate roots for myself out of my current story and discover my DNA so I could unfold into my authenticity. But as a child I didn't know I had lost my mom and dad and my roots; this was only in the background of my awareness. What I knew consciously was I was chosen, adopted, and a member of the K--- family just like everyone else.

I was aware that Mom and Dad loved me. Yet as I grew, the void within me grew too, yelling out for attention, yelling to be filled. It is from this place that I began to develop parallel lives—in the first I lived from my soul, and in the second I tried to be like my family. My childhood was full of omissions, secrets, unrecognized talents and self-created misconceptions: I feel loss but I am chosen. I want to know my ancestors but I love this family I have. As the years passed and small revelations about my birth family leaked out, I began to wonder what was the truth and what have I made up in my own memory?

As I questioned, Who am I? I developed pictures of myself. I had no mirror image to look at, so my self-perceptions were dependent on how my family responded. I wrapped these responses around me as a shield—used them as my looking glass. I tried to make sense out of what I heard. Did it fit with what I felt? The comments I heard don't add up. Everyone told me I am a member of our family just like everyone else; yet I didn't look like anyone in my family. I had different blood, and what did that mean exactly? And for that matter what did it mean to be a member of my family just like everyone else? I knew I was loved but I felt empty too. These incongruences weren't explained. No one ever said, "We're sorry you lost your birth-parents, you must be sad about that." I was simply told I was a chosen child. Or not told that at all.

One of those wounding incidents I remember. I was playing outside with my sisters one day and all of a sudden they began chanting: "You're not a member of our family, you're adopted; you're not a member of our family, you're adopted."

Children can say wounding things; but I was a child, too, and all I understood was the wound itself, not anything about the ones doing the wounding. I ran down the street, bursting with tears, trying to get as far away as possible. A neighbor saw me, stopped short and turned. I registered the kindness in her eyes. I ran to her, the tears streaming down my face, and in a choked voice, I said, and "My sisters say I'm not a member of our family because I'm adopted."

She gently leaned forward and opened her arms; I leaned in, feeling her protection. She stood, holding me tightly, absorbing my tears until I stopped crying. Then she whispered, "You are a very special girl and member of your family; you were chosen to be part of your family. Your sisters were born to your parents, they didn't know whether they would get a girl or boy baby; but you were chosen. Just remember you were chosen to be part of your family and then your sisters' words can't hurt you anymore."

She continued calming me, saying her own daughter was adopted and they were so glad they chose her. "We love her so much. I feel blessed everyday by our sweet daughter. She is one hundred percent a member of our family no matter what."

Fortified with this kindness, I dried my eyes and felt stronger inside knowing I was chosen and special. I went home able to act the whole sister again.

Of course being chosen and special keeps you outside and separate, too, but I didn't know that then. And being chosen sets up an imaginary standard to live up to. If you are special and chosen, you want to do whatever it takes to live up to the expectations of those who choose you.

The kindness of the woman in our neighborhood wasn't out of the normal—in that, I was fortunate, too. Adoption was well accepted in my neighborhood. On our street there were three other adopted children and by the time I was thirteen, there were two more. We all shared our stories. I was the only one who lived with siblings born to their birth parents, however, so my experiences were sometimes different.

On one such occasion when I was eight, I was playing at my best friend's house while she was getting ready to celebrate her adoptive birthday. She and her five-year-old sister had two birthday celebrations each year. They celebrated on the days of their births and on the arrival dates of their adoptions. Wow, I thought, what a great idea! It felt really right to celebrate both dates, to honor the whole truth of being adopted. I could hardly wait to tell my Mom.

I burst into kitchen in total delight, sputtering in my excitement, "Kit's celebrating her adoption birthday today. Can I have an adoption birthday party too?"

My mom simply looked sweetly at me. "Honey you are a full-fledged member our family and we each have one birthday party a year, on our birthday."

I felt crushed that I couldn't celebrate my adoption birthday; it seemed really important to me but I never mentioned it again. Years later, every year the Saturday after Thanksgiving, I remembered my second birthday and honored it myself. This was when I came to live with my new family. I'm not an orphan; I have a home and parents that love me. I don't know if anyone else thought about it, but I still acknowledged this beginning.

Chapter Three: What We Do to Belong—Secondary Wounds

Different but "chosen," I developed beliefs and behaviors to keep myself safe. Sometimes it was safe inside the family; other times, safe within myself. I sensed how to be appropriate in different situations, all designed to fit in and belong. Over time I realized that questions about belonging couldn't be heard by my family because they simply accepted me as part of the unit—when not separating me out. However, I lived in a maze of two parallel lives, a maze filled with distortions, mixed messages, underground feelings, and unanswered questions until I reached my forties. Then I began to unravel the mystery and find my way back to my authentic self. I did this by answering my own questions, connecting and listening to my heart and discovering my soul's truth. I also worked at finding and listening to my inner children's beliefs, which allowed me to heal the distortions and misconceptions developed in early childhood. These were those beliefs:

1. I'm outside looking in, is there a way to connect? How can I do it?
2. I'm chosen and special, but can you see me?
3. I'm adopted and different from my family, but I'm a member of the family just like everyone else.
4. Who am I really? They say I'm creative like Pop, my grandfather, but we don't share blood. How can I be like him?
5. I could have been an orphan on the street. I'm one of the lucky ones. I'd better be good, be grateful and fit in and not make waves.
6. When are you going to leave me? I am afraid you will abandon me if I am too much or too needy.
7. I'm not good enough to belong; I have to prove my worth. I freely give my talents.
8. I have to prove myself, do something to belong.

I had to approach these beliefs consciously and with compassion later in life because being adopted and feeling different had long forced me to find ways to "fit in" with my family. I thought the way to belong was to become like my family. But as I matured I experienced myself less and less like my siblings. I felt more outside, different and misunderstood.

I have, for instance, a natural affinity for beauty, fashion, home design space and nature. Early on, fashion opened my senses to the multiplicity of textures and colors and weights, and I eagerly appreciated a diversity of styles and aesthetics. I can easily see how to change a piece of clothing for an entire new look, from funk to sophistication, or to evoke fun casual. This might seem trivial to some, but playing with fashion provided me with an entire cast of characters for self-discovery. As I discovered more about fashion styles, proportions and colors, it helped me forge deeper connections to my emotional self. I discovered how fashion made me feel: sexy, pretty, sensible, outrageous or flamboyant. Literally I could see myself in the mirror and be connected with the self-reflected back. Fashion gave me a way to express my unique self; for me to discover and appreciate it. I loved the variety of moods that can be expressed through clothing and artistic choices.

Also within me was the innate awareness of home space design. Even at seven years old, I had to move my bedroom furniture around to create mini environments—little places for stories and magical experiences. Out in the world, I mentally re-created environments everywhere I went, re-arranging furniture or art for a new experience. By the time I reached my teens, I sometimes rearranged our living room and family room in addition to my bedroom. I didn't realize it, but my creativity was emerging.

My personal preference is for calm, intriguing spaces filled with light, art and comfortable furnishings that encourage prolonged conversations and peace of mind. Most people appreciate this environment—and I discovered I could create it. Furthermore I like to infuse that space with a sense of the sacred, such as with an altar of favorite things, a glimpse of natural vistas, or the act of bringing the outside world inside in other ways. This treatment of a room allows us to stay connected to the earth and the sky, activating our hearts divinity.

Without the heartbeat of my mother, music keeps my soul alive, awakening my body to the rhythm capturing the musical flow and beat within me. However, until I was older I didn't nurture my true nature. I was focused on fitting in and how to belong and be like my family. For over thirty years I had no idea who my true self was. I was in the business of trying to fit in and belong.

My family's approach to life was different from my nature. It was planned, practical and thought out, an educational process guided by a linear approach. They focused on goals, saved up for what they wanted and obtained their desires one by one. I tried to create beauty and elegance around me at all times even when it cost more, whereas they seemed interested in practical, durable and getting the most for their money. They loved to watch sports, whereas I was mostly interested in the arts.

My family's practical, instrumental approach to life was applied to arts, so I felt the division most keenly there. My mother's idea of dance, for example, was to expose us all too different forms of art—that way, we would be well-rounded individuals. But I loved dance. When I took tap lessons, I learned I was really good. I wanted to continue and pursue my artistic talents as an everyday practice. I craved the wood floor, the sound of the taps, the rhythms inspired me. However, lessons beyond this basic exposure were not part of the overall plan. So I learned tap basics and then dance ended.

Maybe my natural talent just couldn't be seen by Mom. Maybe it was out of her realm of consciousness, outside of her personal DNA. I was the only one interested in dance…no one else in my family was drawn to their lessons.

Meanwhile, dancing and singing were in my blood. I searched for venues. In junior high and high school, I went to all the school dances. I also sat in on my friend's ballet and modern dance classes. I hoped by watching I could learn the steps. Sometimes I asked my friends to teach me their routines and practiced with them. I was named the best dancer in my high school class. I had dreams of being a jazz dancer on stage. I was inspired by Shirley Maclain, Raquel Welch and the dancers in West Side Story and All that Jazz. As an adult, I enrolled in jazz dance classes and weekly private lessons. As a fitness director, I had an opportunity to provide a jazz dance company with a place to practice; they invited me into their workouts. Off and on over the course of my life, I have used dance as a form of exercise. Through dance I was discovering once again my true nature.

Singing, unlike dance, was not easy for me. My voice needed training, so its development remained unattended in my childhood years. When I finally started lessons later in life, I quickly understood I needed to warm up the voice and practice. This isn't strange. Singing uses the voice as an instrument. Warming up coaxes the vocal cords away from everyday sounds into sublime ones.

On a sisterly visit to San Francisco, years after we'd left our childhood home, I shared that I was taking singing lessons. Surprised by this choice, they asked me to sing. With a bit of trepidation I said I would sing one song as a warm up, explaining why, and then sing the three songs I was working on. And as I began, all my sisters laughed. They just laughed.

I could tell I was singing well, yet their laughter continued. It shocked me and brought me back to earlier times when I had not been heard. I felt dishonored and hurt. I wanted to scream, "How dare you" and storm out of the room. But this time I stood my ground I did not abandon myself. Instead, I continued to sing. I sang all three songs, singing them well. I sang to honor me. I was still hurt but at least I knew I could sing no matter what my sisters did. I could sing for my love of singing.

From the outside, there might seem a bit of I'll show you in my actions. I wouldn't be offended; it was often how I dealt with rejection and feelings of disconnection. I learned to push through when there was no feedback or negative feedback; it was a matter of survival a way to show myself I could overcome the adversity and just do it. In this particular case, however, I wanted to sing, to sing because I loved singing. After the songs were sung, however, I was left with the familiar questions of how could they be so cruel? Why did they laugh? Would we as sisters ever understand each other? Can I ever be appreciated just for who I am?

Chapter Four: Divided Self, Divided Language

As a teen, I was painfully aware each night during dinner conversation around the dining room table that I was different. Dancing, singing and design were not the only differences. Language itself was an obstacle course I couldn't get through. It was customary for us to eat our dinner together, and over the meal we would have discussions on a variety of subjects—the older sister's French lessons, current events, and whatever was happening with each of us. Frequently when it was my turn, I used the wrong word in place of another word. Malapropism was my nemesis. I couldn't keep an idiom straight. Whenever it happened, everyone laughed, corrected me and moved on. Most of the time I didn't get the joke, I was confused and unaware of my error. I did not get the distinction between the word I used and the correct word and was not quite sure what had actually transpired. I noticed how this was only something that happened to me. It reinforced my feelings of being different, separate and alone.

My sisters said I was dumb. For a long time, I believed them. I began to test my intelligence. I had adult conversations with the neighbors. They seem to acknowledge my intelligence.

I also had difficulty spelling and no one else in my family had difficulty spelling. A mild form of dyslexia contributed to both my malapropism and my spelling difficulties—but of course no one knew this. It was just another way I was significantly different.

What would the experience of speaking and writing have been like had I known I wasn't alone? What if a blood relation also had difficulties with word and idiom choices? Had difficulty with spelling? Does my DNA have this answer?

Without the DNA knowledge, however, these areas of difference were seen as unique to me—and the assumed cause was lack of intelligence. People weren't tested for learning disabilities when I grew up. They were judged by each other's abilities instead.

Reading was a particularly haunting example of this in our family. My sisters read volumes of books for pleasure. I on the other hand was much more interested in doing anything active.

I developed an affinity for reading in my late twenties. But in fifth grade I was put in a remedial reading class after being shamed by the teacher for having difficulty reading aloud. I could read silently, but I just couldn't sound out all the words. Sometimes I had difficulty with reading comprehension. I had difficulty with multiple-choice questions because it was hard to find the distinctions between the multiple-choice answers. I had no problem with open expression or essay tests. This is typical dyslexic behavior but since I was unaware of dyslexia, it was again simply attributed to my lack of intelligence by my teachers and family.

I believed from fifth grade forward that I couldn't read, considering myself a remedial reader and less accomplished/bright than my classmates. This affected my self-esteem and I resisted involvement in any activity for which I had to read aloud. I stopped trying out for plays, for instance. I built a wall of fear between reading and me, so much so that if I were asked to read aloud, the words would blur when I looked at the page. If I were being tested on reading, I would simply pretend to read and zone out, pick multiple-choice answers randomly. Even as an adult, I panicked and heard absolutely nothing if a seminar leader randomly called on someone to read. I heard I was a remedial reader and I took it on as my truth. Out of this misconception I created myself as a non-reader. Within me grew no explanation for how I could be so smart and such a quick study, yet have so much difficulty reading aloud.

Then in my mid-forties came along a kind boyfriend whose custom was to read aloud to me. His reading touched me and opened a desire to reciprocate. It was time to heal my fears of reading aloud. I was open to any venue that could make this happen. At this time in my life I had developed and facilitated a seminar I called The Empowerment Course. I decided this was the perfect venue for me to overcome my fear of reading aloud. I decided to read aloud at the beginning of each weekly class to reclaim this power. I choose readings that would enhance and set the tone for each class and I explained to my class my fear of reading aloud and asked them to hold loving space for me to reclaim my power, which I had shut down for nearly twenty years. It worked; I truly enjoy reading aloud now. It has become a pleasure.

But the divisions continue to exist between the language of my family and the language I speak. My mom being an English teacher, the **proper** use of language was uniquely important to my family. In my early forties, while visiting my mom on holiday, I was asked to explain my consulting work. I began by telling her I did "Visioning." She and my sister quickly cut in. "Visioning," I was told, "is not a verb—you cannot use it in this way."

Undeterred, I began to explain the process. "Visioning—"

Mom interrupted me again. "Visioning is not a verb. Please refrain from using this term in this manner before you continue." At this point I shut down; I didn't know quite how proceed. How could I explain this new work I called Visioning without using the word? To me it said it all.

I asked, "Do you want to hear about what I'm doing now or do you want to argue about the proper use of words?"

They replied in unison, "When you can use the word vision properly, we can continue with your work story."

I was frustrated and disappointed. Visioning soon would become a widely used term in Corporate America to explain the part of a process helping people to look into the future. Sadly, I was never able to explain this work to my family. Their critical analysis was not only directed at me but at any misuse of language by anyone. This experience once again reinforced that I was unable to be heard or be a true full member of the family.

I found myself full of anger and I withdrew completely. When I was not understood or heard, it triggered me back to a place before words. I had to calm myself before returning to my adult person. So I turned my Walkman up to the maximum and went off to pout like I had done as a child. Neither my sister nor my mom seemed to know what to do. When I returned to the room, the subject was simply dropped. The pattern continued over the years. I would speak and use the wrong word or use a word incorrectly, triggering my family to resist and stop listening. When I was not heard I would shut down. After years of this pattern, I began to withhold information I felt they could not hear, which *guaranteed* I wasn't heard. This resulted in many lost opportunities to connect, communicate and truly share my life fully with my family.

The odd thing about these fundamental differences between my family and myself in matters of language and in art is how, essentially, my adopted family did not see them. I might be considered lacking in intelligence, but any talent worth celebrating brought me immediately into the fold. "You're just like Pop," my father would say, speaking about his father. "That's where your talent comes from."

Most certainly, I admired Pop's creativity. He wrote in his journal each day, his poems and stories were published, and he designed and built a half-dozen homes that to me exuded strong and unique presences. I was flattered each time I was told my creativity came from Pop, but I knew his blood was not my blood. How, then, could I still be like him? I appreciated all his talents but I continued to ask where my talent comes from?

I tried to have this conversation with my family, but they'd just look at me and say, "We just told you, you're like Pop. You have his creativeness; you get your talent from him. You're part of our family just like the rest of us." These conversations were confusing, and because of this confusion within me, I didn't feel my family even saw *me*. As a result, I was preoccupied with where my talent came from and I missed hearing their acknowledgments. I sometimes couldn't feel or hear my families support because I was living a parallel life created by my internal questioning. So I began to feel unheard, outside, alone and disconnected—yet chosen.

Chapter Five: Are You My Brother?

Due to these struggles and early confusion, I created beliefs that I lived out most of my life. As I deepened into myself and found my truth, my earlier beliefs shifted. Slowly I began to uncover the truth of my authentic self. Like most of us, we spend our lives caught in our misconceptions and distortions until something wakes us up and we become conscious. Then we look for ways to return to our true nature, to our essential self.

But first comes the times of inner confusion—of awkward choices and even the loss of one's truth.

When it was time for applying to college, my family encouraged me to go into a retail internship instead. This, in actuality, supported my true gifts—but that's not what I heard. My interpretation was that they felt I was not smart enough to go to college. So, to fit in and be like my siblings, I was determined to go to college and show them I could do it.

Just like many other teenagers, I took a job before heading off into my new life. It was at this juncture that my foundation was knocked off center.

"Are you adopted?"

Between high school and college, I worked for a year for a local engineering company as a file clerk. One day I was filing items in the blue-print department, and I glanced up to find this man looking at me very closely.

He asked his question with such sincerity, I answered without much hesitation. "Yes, I am adopted, why do you ask?"

He led me over to his desk and handed me a black-and-white photo of a woman in a small 3 x 5 silver frame. Her eyes, nose and mouth looked back at me as if I was looking in the mirror. She really looked like me. It was spooky and exciting. I had never seen anyone who resembled me before.

He said, "This is a picture of my sister. I have two brothers and a sister, and our youngest sister was put up for adoption. I thought you might be her. Ever since you came to work here, I noticed you, and you look so much like my sister that ... maybe I might be your brother."

My heart raced; I was deeply shaken and excited. This man standing directly in front of me might actually be my brother. Oh my God! I'd never really given him a look before, but now I stood still and looked into his green-blue eyes, so much like my own. I noticed his mouth with the full bottom lip and his straight nose similar to mine and our hair the same color of rich golden brown. He stood taller than me with a strong, comforting build.

I began to question him: "Tell me how come your sister was given away? How old are you and your brother and sister? Where are you from? Tell me your whole story … please."

He told the story. "When I was a little boy, my dad was killed in the war and my mom was very poor. She was afraid the government would come and take all of us away. She sent my younger sister to live with relatives and raised my brother and me; soon after, she put our baby sister up for adoption."

This story was so similar to the one I had heard as a child … could it be true? I was anxious to get home and check things out, find out my birth last name, where I was actually born, and where I had come from? Could this man, standing right next to me, be my brother? All these thoughts raced through my brain. By the time I arrived home, I was wound up like a top waiting to be set free.

I ran into the house to tell my mom this news. As I spoke, however, disappointment edged with fear became imprinted on her normally open face. Yet she listened and told me what she knew. She spoke my birth last name for the first time: "L-----." It did not match the name of the man I worked with.

She spoke softly, saying she was sorry he wasn't my brother. She also expressed surprise that I wanted to find by birth family. After witnessing her reaction to the possibility of finding a sibling, I felt it somehow unsafe or uncaring of me to search for my birth relatives. I dropped the whole inquiry. Like other choices I had made previously, such as whether to go to traditional college or into fashion design, I choose the safe road the one the family would understand. I told myself I could have been an orphan; I needed to fit in and be grateful for what I have. If it upset my mother to find my birth family, it wasn't worth it. My inner drive to be part of my adoptive family was most important. To fit in and be like everyone else won out—I suppressed my deeper need to be true to myself. At the time I had no idea how this suppression was shaping my life.

Today I wonder if the man at the engineering company is my brother after all. The name on my birth records could have been my birth mom's maiden name, who knows? I've been unsuccessful in finding any of my siblings yet.

Chapter Six: The Passport Experience—Triggers from the past

I'm twenty-nine, burnt out, and ready for a vacation. I've married a man with three children and spent the last year opening and staffing a new YMCA aquatic facility. It's February and the temperature registers in the low teens with no warmth in sight. I dream of flying away to the tropical paradise of the French Caribbean. There is one small glitch. I need a passport and I don't have one. So, I'm off to the local post office to apply for one.

I arrive at the post office; it's fairly empty of customers. I easily find the passport forms and fill them out. Then to the counter I go with forms in hand, along with my current driver's license, a certificate of birth, and a check for the passport processing fee.

I greet John, the postal employee, with a smile. "Hi, how are you today? I've come to apply for a passport. Here are my documents and a check."

He examines all the paperwork and then to my surprise, hands everything back to me. "You must be adopted. You get a *certificate of birth*—not a *birth certificate*—when you're adopted. A certificate of birth is unacceptable when filing for a passport. You must bring in your adoption papers to prove who you are and that you are an American citizen."

Thankful no one else listened to this exchange. I stand there in quiet shock, unable to speak, but my thoughts are racing. This certificate was okay for school, for my driver's license, and everything else I can remember. In one simple statement—*this certificate of birth is unacceptable when filing for a passport*—I feel my whole identity is questioned. What is the difference between a birth certificate and a certificate of birth anyway; the only thing different to me is that the words are reversed. It's mind-blowing.

I collect myself as best I can and turn away, wondering what it will be like to ask my mother for my adoption papers. Will asking upset my parents? The last time I talked with Mom about being adopted was when I thought I met my birth brother, and she was not pleased. In fact, she was shaken. Her relief that the last names weren't a match stopped me from searching for my family roots. I didn't want to upset the ones who had chosen me and given me love, who'd given me a warm home and lots of opportunities in life. And now I had to bring up the adoption again, a topic we never discuss.

Hoping Mom still knows where the adoption papers are, I step away. John interrupts my thoughts—he's still talking … I pull myself back to listen.

"You know, there was a guy in here last week with a certificate of birth and he didn't know he was adopted until I told him. He was forty years old and when I told him he was really freaked out. Ha, Ha!"

Anger rises in me. I feel great empathy for the stranger treated with so much insensitivity. A simple trip to the post office to apply for a passport was turning into something altogether different.

What would I have done if my parents were dead or if I hadn't known I was adopted? Shit, I would really be freaked out. What if they don't know where my adoption papers are? I brace myself for the next step: to ask my mother. I feel turned upside-down and my stomach aches. I wonder what the papers will say about my past. How will this new information affect me? I feel as if I'm transported back-wards to my time of birth, when I was without words. At the same time, I know in my head somewhere, all I really want is to be on vacation.

I drive to my Mom's house, expectations building alongside a low guttural panic, preparing my words and trying to stay calm. She's home.

Nervously I tell her the situation. "Mom, I've planned a trip to the Caribbean next month, and the travel agency informed me today that I need a passport. I went to the post office this morning and they wouldn't accept my certificate of birth as proof that I am an American citizen. They say I need to bring in my adoption pa-pers to prove who I am."

I'm tight as a stretched-out rubber band, muscles tense, as I look with anticipa-tion at her. She just nods and smiles sweetly. "I will get the papers for you."

Nonchalantly, she beckons me to follow her upstairs to her bedroom. My im-mediate fear of securing the papers is erased. She retrieves my adoption papers from Dad's dresser. I'm amazed to find they were there all the time in the small top right-hand drawer. Then, lightly with love, she hands the envelope over to me.

Briefly I look into my Mom's kind, round face; I notice her rosy cheeks and her soft hazel eyes. I'm touched and scared at the same time. I know somewhere inside that I'm about to find out and see a little bit of my past …. I realize I'm holding my breath and I let out a sigh.

I don't know why, I have no words to explain it, but I can't open the envelope right away. My chest is tight, I must remind myself to breathe, breathe. I hug my mom tightly, and with tears and a kiss I simply say thanks. We make our way downstairs to the kitchen, we hug again, and without knowing how I got there, I'm back in my car.

As I drive away from my childhood home, I know somewhere inside that I need to look at these papers alone. I don't want my mother's reactions mixed into what I will find. Mom and I rarely discussed intimate issues with each other, and besides, I need time to digest all that has happened this morning. There is time to look inside the brown, weathered envelope; it can wait until I get home. The magnitude of all that has happened is not quite registering. But I do know this has been some kind of powerful day.

I'm filled with so many contradictory feelings. I've never asked to see my adoption papers. In the past asking questions about my adoption was met with mixed reactions. In a way, I'm frustrated that this situation even came up. I find myself boomeranged back into the place of emotions without words; it's frightening and frustrating trying to make sense of myself. All my life I've been an American citizen and now I have to prove it because I'm adopted. Deep within me I'm scared to look at the papers. What will I learn new about myself or my birth family—and how will this affect me now?

For an hour or so, I wander aimlessly around my house trying to settle down. Then in the privacy of my bedroom, I hold the envelope in my hands. With anticipation I open it. I pull out the brown, aged papers. Unfolding them carefully I begin to read:

> State of Michigan, The Probate Court for the County of Oakland, on the 7th day of January 1946. Present: Honorable Arthur E. Moore, Judge of Probate. In the Matter of Cheryle Anne L----, Order of Adoption Confirmation. A petition having been duly filed in this cause by Charles K. and Elizabeth K. petitioners, praying that an order may be entered decreeing that said child be legally adopted by said petitioners, and the child thereof, and decreeing that the child's name be changed to Martha Jane K.

For the first time I see my birth name. I repeat it to myself "Cheryle Anne, Cheryle Anne." It sounds delicious to me, I like it—it seems to fit me better. I've never really felt like a Martha Jane. I wish my name was not changed.

I read further. The document lists adoption approval from the hospital where I was born, as well as an adoption consent and release by the social worker assigned to my case. The paper concludes with approval and order that my new mom and dad "stand in the place of said parents" and that my name be changed to Martha Jane K. The document is signed by the judge.

I work my way through the documents. I come across a hospital form stating my name, birth date, and then, in the next line, there before my eyes, I see for the very first time, my birthmother's name. *Doris L----, age 23.*

I sit transfixed. This is my mom's name? Her first and last name? I try to take her name into me; maybe in her name I can feel her, know her in some small way. Taking in these new names sends my physical body reeling. Looking at these papers I feel a longing to know my mom once again.

As I move down the form, next I discover my birth weight listed at 5.2lbs. I wonder why I only weighed 5.2 pounds—was I premature? Next the form lists my feeding schedule; it says I was breast fed for one month. Did my Mom feed me or did a wet nurse? Once again in my life, more unanswered questions. The form ends by saying I'm healthy and ready for adoption. At my hospital release, I weighed 8.11 lbs.

I read on through the papers, through letters of agreement between my parents and the social worker stating that I be placed in my parents' home as if in foster care for one year while they are evaluated as suitable parents. It appears this one-year process is the typical waiting period. It seems like a long time to put parents and infant on hold. And what happens to the bonding process during this period of time—especially when the mother becomes pregnant so soon after?

There are more letters filing for petitions for adoption, questions and correspondence between my parents and the case worker, and one requesting personal character references, with a return reference attached. As I finish reading through these documents, I take in just how much disclosure was requested of my parents and how vulnerable they have been as they tried to adopt me and bring me into their home. In the mist of this discovery, I immediately have a new appreciation for my parents and their part in the adoption journey. Feelings of gratefulness once more flood over me.

I remember this discovery began with a simple trip to the post office to apply for a passport. It triggered a retreat back in time to my birth, a time without words and with lots of feelings. In one short day I discovered my birthmother's name, my birth weight and whatever that means, and the adoptive journey of my adoptive parents—and I am still in need of a passport.

The next day, still somewhat numb, I drive back to the post office with all my documents and a copy of my adoption papers. Once again John greets me, this time with a simple nod.

"I'm back to apply for a passport," I say. "I have my adoption papers and all the other necessary documents with me."

It is uneventful. John barely acknowledges me or my adoption papers; he simply flips through the documents, nods, takes my check and puts them all in a large white envelope, seals it, stamps it and tosses it in the bin for pick-up. "You should get your new passport in the mail in about three weeks." My passport arrives just in time for my trip.

The French Caribbean is all that I dreamed it would be, the temperature a constant eight-five degrees, the water crystal clear and aqua blue with warm trade breezes. I feel my feet in the sand as I run along the white sand beach in early morning. It is so peaceful here, the sun is beginning to rise and soon it will be warm. I make my way back to the hotel for breakfast and on my way I think about the journey that got me here. I feel changed immeasurably and moved by all that I have learned, glad to be alive and well. Being here on vacation on this beautiful stretch of beach in the sun seems to heal the shock ripples of getting my adoption papers. The quiet and the sun warm my soul for the time being.

But, this adoption process is a never-ending journey of healing. It takes me by the shoulders and shakes me, turning me upside down when I least expect it. Twenty-some years later as I sit down to write this chapter, I realize I still have this same unanswered question: why is a certificate of birth unacceptable in proving citizenship or applying for a US passport?

I'd like to put this question to rest. The lack of knowledge brings to the surface another layer of frustration and anger for me to heal. I contact the US Passport Office and a variety of adoption agencies with inquiries. But after two full days on the phone, hearing mostly recorded messages, unable to make personal contact or even get a person to correspond with in writing, I give up. I did reach one person at an adoption agency, but she could not explain to me why the Certificate of Birth was unacceptable in applying for a passport or in proving citizenship. I did find out children adopted from other countries are given a green card, and at the time of their adoption they become legal citizens of the US and are issued a new birth certificate. US-born children who are relinquished and adopted, to protect the rights of their birthparents and the security/secrecy of their adoptive parents, have their birth certificate and all historical information withheld from them. They issue a certificate of birth in place of a birth certificate. My birth records are still sealed, along with my history.

When I get to these places, places without answers, I remember why it's so hard to write this book. I get angry at the constant injustice and lack of sensitivity that is present when you ask questions about adoption. The regular response is writing a letter to… And request information on… or fill out this form and submit it with a check for….. Or have you filed here or registered there … *Nothing* is immediate or straightforward. Over time it wears you down, so little progress is made. For me it seems most productive to live in the present, be in life, but the past keeps showing up, to be dealt with. I've let go of knowing my history over and over again, and then a spurt of anger will catch me and I'm off again asking unanswered questions. The fact is I seldom get complete answers to my history and so much is unknown, so the feelings associated with the lack of information never goes away. The feelings of frustration, hurt, sadness, and anger sit there under the surface, just waiting to be triggered by anything similar to my loss and confusion from being adopted. These triggered emotions surface during times of happiness and loss. Being conscious and healing my earlier wounds is my way through them.

None of my correspondence to the US Passport Office has ever been answered. It is time to let go of my hurt, disguised as injustice, and move on. As long as I am incomplete and without my past, there is likelihood that my emotions will be triggered, but what I do in the face of these triggers is the journey. Each time I confront my demons, they shrink and I become more of who I am.

I can feel my feelings and use this energy in some productive way. I can just feel my feelings and appreciate knowing nothing is perfect and simply let go. I can choose to have compassion for myself and for everyone involved in the adoption process, understanding it is complex. I can simply realize that each experience, and how I handle it, is a step in my evolution as a spiritual being, holding greater and greater compassion for others and for myself on the journey. Completing one particular situation does not mean I will not be triggered again by another similar event, but each time, I learn another element of letting go. I also re-evaluate what is important to me, which brings me back to my authentic self, a place I want to know and be.

Chapter Seven: Bringing It All Together

All my early longings are now integrated into my life. My essential self has emerged despite feelings of being separate, alone, abandoned and despite some paths I have chosen. I have become whole, and that wholeness is reflected in what I do. This includes the things most challenging to hold close.

In my past, feelings of being outside a group and trying to get in help create a pattern regarding chosen people and situations. I married a man with three children, for instance, and yet felt outside the core family unit. This was a recreation of my adoptive family story.

My past influenced patterns in my business life as well. I chose to be a business consultant, entering businesses from the vantage point of an unbiased outsider. I provided a forum for others that fostered free communication and stronger relationships; I facilitated partnerships and team development. Likewise, I assisted clients as they uncovered solutions for complex situations. I was a needed witness but essentially separate.

When I partnered with my clients as a healer, my role once again was to hold sacred space for healing. In our sessions I would listen to a person's story and assist in healing surfaced trauma, but I remained detached from their outcome. My role was to help each client to walk on her or his own (spirit) path, while I stayed on mine. I remained present, and I held each client in unconditional love and I honored where they are in their process. I facilitated clearing whatever was in the way of them coming into balance. I introduced them to ways to find their own truth, their Divinity heart-wisdom, their soul's journey—then they chose how to proceed down their path.

To heal my own story, I continue to work on expanding my short-term intimate relationships into deeper long-term ones. It is easy for me to connect with people quickly; it is easy to create intimate short-term relationships. In my past I would connect with people and get out before finding out if I really belonged. In personal relationships I am aware that I must be diligently conscious to speak my truth so that I don't fall into the old beliefs of feeling outside that creates disconnections.

The stories shared here in Part One illustrate what unresolved abandonment looks like throughout different stages of life and how confusing it can be for a young child. My family modeled their view of life out of what nourished and sustained them. They did what they knew to do to preserve their knowing. Being adopted is different. Finding my inner truth through the forest of misconceptions has been my spiritual gateway home to my essential self.

PART TWO

Journey of Triggers & Healings

Introduction

In 1985 my marriage of fourteen years comes to an end, and I have moved into a condo in the Galleria area of Houston. My spiritual journey is in full expansion and I am deepening into my fuller self. A few years later, in 1988, I attend a National Organization Transformation Conference where I meet a group of leading-edge consultants. They are excited about my work, confirming its uniqueness. They inform me that the elements of my practice are exactly what companies are looking for on the west coast. So in 1989, I move from Houston, Texas, to San Francisco, California, to begin a new chapter in my life.

My high expectations are soon realized—this move opens the doors to new and exciting opportunities to partner with other like-minded consultants, providing new avenues to expand my consulting practice. The Bay Area is alive with business leaders exploring new forms of leadership and I am in this mix. We assist company leaders to view their businesses and their roles within them from an expanded view, using mind, body and spirit. I take leaders into themselves via guided meditations as they begin "Visioning" their company into the future. I work with them from the inside-out to assist them in seeing and experiencing who they need to be within themselves to lead their company forward. I coin the phrase for this work—Executive Coaching—well before it becomes a standard practice across the United States.

During this time period, my personal life is strained. I begin to feel more and more overwhelmed and out of balance without knowing why. My practice is thriving but it is time now to heal my early childhood wounds. I've discovered I have abandonment issues and have begun early childhood development therapy. In therapy I am asked where I was before being adopted. Back home, I ask Mom, who tells me I spent the first three months of my life in the hospital alone without my mother. I determine in this moment to take care of myself. My infant self is trying to take care of me, which is causing my feelings of being overwhelmed. Other more hidden aspects of myself surface, in need of healing.

Beyond traditional therapy I continue to stretch myself and to experience other forms of healing. I take a year-long course in Alchemical Hypnotherapy, as well as intensive courses in Watsu Massage. This adds to my skill base as a personal coach and later as a healer.

I remember reading about Lynn Andrew's spiritual dreaming retreats and her Native teachers. She would dream her way into the sacred of the Medicine Wheel. This is a form I am ready to try. To create this experience I contact a friend from my past, a woman I met in Houston who attended our fire walk. She lives in Santa Rosa, California,about an hour north of San Francisco. I ask her and her friend to create a spiritual retreat for me. I am ready to drop in deeper to my spiritual knowing, to renew and nourish myself.

Even though my life is filled with joy, deep connections and success, living in the shadows are unanswered questions, sadness and a longing for fullness. The tension between success and personal strain is palpable.

This section of PULLING ON NEW GENES identifies healing times that shine light into the shadows, capturing the triggers leading to underlying disturbances. I present them in short vignettes to allow you, the reader, to see and experience the early childhood wounds and the process of healing. As you will see, disturbances reoccur on the spiritual path, and this is nothing to be ashamed of or frightened by. Over time things surface again and again until we have completed the healing for each particular trigger.

Chapter Eight: Healing My Inner Child—Newborn to Three

In the summer of 1991, I scheduled a Spiritual Retreat with two healer friends. After a string of busy months with my consulting practice as an executive coach, I realize I need time to focus and replenish and renew my own spiritual journey. Working in corporate America is exciting, but it uses a lot of energy. So I contact these two friends and ask if, together, they would assist me on this quest.

The weekend of the retreat, my friends greet me with hugs and smiles. Grace and Star, both of whom I know well and trust. They are Native American Pipe Carriers and know the way of creating a sacred circle and praying to the Great Spirit. We have done ritual together over many years, each time as rewarding as the last.

They show me to my room. Next to the bed is a small table draped with a cloth and covered with an assortment of quartz crystals and other minerals. These release their sweet energies into my dream space. The room feels fresh and clean. A lavender bedspread throws its restful color against the walls and furniture, enhancing my inner journey and dreaming. I unpack and arrange things, preparing myself with a few deep breaths before joining my friends and retreat guides in the living room. It's time to share where we each are, and where we are headed together.

I read my goals for the retreat. They listen deeply and acknowledge my desires. They state they are in alignment with all my intentions, thanking me for my clarity.

They begin by asking me to choose a younger age, to role-play. I choose seventeen. In unison they tell me no; instead, could I pick an age under three? I am repulsed; I've never liked young children, particularly under the age of three.

Ignoring my resistance, Grace and Star become young children right in front of me—crawling on the floor, curious of their surroundings, checking out everything directly in front of them. Their actions and expressions demonstrate children around the ages of 1 ½ and 2 years old respectively. Disgusted and extremely uncomfortable, I silently watch them carry out their charade. They play off of one another, grabbing things and talking in baby talk. "Mine," one yells, as she grabs a stuffed rabbit from the other. The other cries, "Smorry," her bottom lip in a pout. By this time I am furious. I've come here for an *adult* retreat and they are acting like whiny children.

Star starts to cry. Despite my cringing, I find myself asking, "Can I help you, little one. It seems to me that you need some love and attention." She immediately assents.

As I begin to comfort her, I move down onto the floor and reach out. With this gesture, my two colleagues become adults, and they begin to nurture me. And as they coddle and stroke, I seem to become small and child-like. The trickster has come to call.

Trickster medicine is the humor of the ages—the great cosmic joke. When you are caught in your own foolishness the trickster has come to call. Star and Grace set up this ruse so they could trick me into becoming my younger self. To protect the vulnerable younger parts of myself, I stay as an adult as much as possible—but trickster medicine is tricky to avoid.

Grace situates herself behind me and wraps her arms around my body, cradling me, rocking me gently side to side. She speaks softly into my ear, as if speaking to a very young child. "It's okay, young one, we are here, we are here with you, and we love you and welcome you here." I begin to cry, tears streaming down my face. She brushes them away gently like a mother.

This is exactly what my inner younger self needs. Immediately I breathe and relax, and this nurturance slips in. Then Star begins noticing the qualities of my body, like one might with a newborn child. Both pat my head, look closely at my hands and feet, all the while commenting to each other on each body part. "Such beautiful well-formed hands she has, they will bring great healing into the world. They will know how to plant seeds and pull the weeds when they get to thick, strong hands this is good… Look at her feet each toe perfectly formed, beautiful feet for walking and carrying her through life, yes, this is good. Her head is so sweet, her eyes so bright, yes, a sweet one indeed…"

Together they move from limb to limb. It feels like a rhythmic massage, leaving me touched and blessed and physically acknowledged from head to toe. I give myself over to them completely. I listen to each word closely, taking in its vibration and its acknowledgment of my beauty. I feel their skilled and loving healing touch as they move their hands from toe to head; I become one with myself, into a newness and vulnerability of just being born, my whole body sucking in these feelings of wonder and love until I feel full. Then very gently they assist me up off the floor and lead to my room for a nap. Feeling full and nourished, I sleep until dinner.

During the entire retreat I remain with my infant self. My cells and core self-seem to take in this nurturing. I have no chores; the only rule is to remain as an infant and be taken care of. I receive delicious meals, I am pampered, and my infant is totally met. I eat, sleep and play.

To enhance my spiritual connection, the second afternoon of the retreat, they gift me with beautiful leather, feathers and other art supplies to create spiritual art. First, I create a ceremonial leather pouch to carry my sacred items—special crystals, feathers, animal bones, river rock—things I have a particular connection to, items that support me in creating sacred ceremony. Next, I make a medicine shield, representing heaven and earth and my connection to my journey. My last creation is an altar cloth made from a rabbit skin and painted on the smooth side with Kokoppelli, the wandering god of futility playing his flute. I affix quartz crystal chips to energize my journey and sew on a beaded medicine wheel to honor the way I have chosen for my journey. As I create these pieces, I feel my deep connection to spirit and am grateful for this sacred creating time—as well as this opportunity to reach into my inner wisdom and remember again who I am.

At the end of each day, my friends tell me stories and tuck me into bed, placing tender kisses on each cheek and sending me off to sleep with the angels. I'm encouraged to remember my dreams so that I can tell their stories in the morning.

All of these nurturing touches touch places deep within me, filling me with experiences that I have never received before. I am heard and seen in ways for which I have always longed. Each day as I nap, I feel myself becoming more and more aligned and balanced. In my meditations I am fully connected to the wonder of the universe, God and all living things.

Adding to this spiritual connection, just before or after my afternoon nap, I play and dig in the rich black dirt of the vegetable garden. Without realizing it, I am covered up to my elbows in dirt; it feels so good to just have my hands and arms in the earth. I have been unconscious of just how disconnected from the earth I have become by working in cement cities and granite buildings, with only patches of landscaped gardens around. Digging in the earth brings me home and roots me into the earth and her beauty.

I'm reminded of my childhood plantings and our family vegetable garden behind our garage. We all planted something; it was a family affair. We planted sweet corn, lettuce, green beans, green onions, carrots, beefsteak tomatoes, and radishes, with marigolds all around the edges to keep the bugs from the new vegetables. I loved to watch the young shoots of new growth peek their heads above the soil. I loved tending the garden; weeding, watering and watching it all grow enjoying the miracle of growth.

Star nudges me and I'm pulled back from my childhood dreaming. She hands over seeds for planting. "Oh boy, yes," I mutter to myself. I carefully plant corn kernels in the soil, cover them over and add water from the hose. I plant beans and lettuce and tomatoes. I bless them all and ask the elements to grow them well. Then the creek calls. I walk down to the creek's edge and sit down on the grass. It's cooler here out of the direct sun; the trees filter the light, and it is so restful. In childhood wonder, sitting transfixed all afternoon by the running stream, I listen to the gentle gurgle of the stream. I have no words, just the sense of being connected with everything without doing anything.

I was looking for a deeper connection to my spirit. What I found was a deeper connection to me, a deeper connection to the earth and ultimately my spirit journey home.

Chapter Nine: The Opening to My Core Childhood Wounds

About a year after my retreat, my boyfriend walked out. A part of me crashed. For the first three days, I was like a caged animal. I had no words—was unsure what was going on. I still worked—I was professional—I stuffed my feelings as best I could. I surrounded myself with friends. But at night, I was so afraid to be alone; I went to my closest friend's home. I couldn't sleep without the presence of another body in the bed to feel safe.

Six months later, hiking with my friend Nicole P. who worked as a therapist, we took a break. We sat in the high yellow grasses of Sonoma County, overlooking a small lake, and then she surprised me by speaking about my early childhood wounding.

"I know you to be really strong and successful," she said not unkindly, "but within you is a large hole and you really need to find someone to work with you to heal it. I'm your friend and I'm not able as your friend to be your therapist."

I felt crushed and embarrassed. My secret was out. I couldn't hide my heart wound any longer. After a few minutes I found my voice and asked whom she would recommend? Is there a specialty I need? She recommended I find someone who works with early childhood development—that my wounds are rooted there.

For at least six months following this conversation I found it hard to be around Nicole. Before this talk we did everything together. Now, I was embarrassed by her observations. The truth of her statements ran deep and touched into my core. I thought I had healed this old wound. But there it gaped, open and visible.

I found a therapist to work with. Nicole's observations and truth were an opening that changed my life. I will always be grateful for her awareness and strength to speak it aloud. Thank you.

Chapter Ten: Push & Pull, Healing My Seven-Year-Old Self

I just feel repulsed by her, her long legs hang out of her khaki shorts like two straight sticks. She really isn't very likable. She is sulky and skinny. I think, "I don't want to know her, I don't want to invite her back—look at her. Yuck."

In a therapy session I discover this seven-year-old part of me that has split off, our energies separated. Whenever she makes herself known to me, I send her away. She embarrasses me. I spend years wishing she would not act out and just leave. I push her to the side, and each time I don't recognize her because she gets uglier and uglier. I can't put my finger on why I keep up the pushing. All I really know is she is skinny and ugly.

When I finally try to reach out to her, she turns her back and goes away. I have forgotten I turned away from her for years. I held her as the ugly one that I didn't want to have anything to do with. I haven't acknowledged her. When this awareness finally hits me, it is as if I have moved a mountain.

I sit quietly and ask this seven-year-old part of me to come and talk with me. I begin to apologize, I begin to see who she is, I begin to honor her just the way she is, and I begin to honor her as part of me. I reach out with welcome. I tell her, without her neither of us is whole. I ask her if she would please come back to me and tell me what will make her happy, what she needs from me to heal.

Slowly over a few years and many times of sitting and listening to this part of my self, she begins to trust me and comes for visits. Then one day we become one again.

Chapter Eleven: A Journey Home to Tell the Truth

In therapy, I am uncovering my childhood journey and learning about my early childhood losses. In the process, I discover I have been holding a secret from my adoptive family. The energy of this secret keeps me separate from them. I have openly shared my story with my friends and lovers since my daughter's birth, that I had a child whom I put up for adoption. However, I kept this information from my adoptive family, something I was totally unaware of until it surfaced in therapy. This omission feels like a bomb just waiting to explode. I feel out of integrity, scuzzy.

There were so many times I couldn't speak my truth. I visited my sister within the year of her daughter's birth. My niece was born February 10, 1966; my daughter was born in September 1966, seven months later. I had to pretend I never had a daughter when my sister said, "Wait till you have a child of your own, it's such a great joy to hold your child." I spaced out and tried to act nonchalant, my insides churning, my heart crying out, "Where's my daughter, I hope she is okay and loved."

When I was pregnant, I lived out of state. To keep the knowledge to myself, I turned down a visit from parents. I felt too ashamed. Out of my shame and fear of what they would do with this information, I missed out on their support and love when I needed it most. I felt I couldn't trust telling them. Would I be the bad girl? Would they abandon me?

It is time now to tell the truth, to find opportunity to rekindle our relationship and to forge a closer connection. Still, I am fearful. How can I tell the truth after all these years and what will happen if I do? I still experience the shame and guilt, feelings I hoped to avoid by not telling my family in the first place. The same things that were present when I was pregnant now confront me. All my life I wanted my parents to be proud of me. Is this why I have held onto this secret? Will they abandon me? Will I be considered good enough to still be part of my family?

With support from my therapist, I make plans to go home and tell Mom. My dad has passed on. I send a letter to my Mom to prepare her. I tell her I am coming home with exciting news. I ask what's the best time to visit—the time when she can set aside time for us to talk without interruptions. I feel this prepares her for our talk.

When I arrive, there is no mention of my letter or any inquiry about my news. There is no opening for discussion. It's as if I'd not written a letter. Furthermore, it seems Mom is avoiding the situation. Whenever there's an opening, I say, "This seems like a good time/place to for our talk—" But Mom changes the subject, gets up and busies herself with something, or suggests we go someplace other than where we are. Other times she simply acts as if she's not heard me.

At one point she suggests we go for a walk. I go from scared to frustrated. I came all this way and I'll never get the truth out. Maybe this is good—I can just run away. But that isn't the answer. My mom definitely isn't making it easy for me.

My week at home draws to an end and I still haven't told my story. It's now the last night of my visit and in fifteen minutes my two nephews and niece are coming for dinner. My tension is maxed out; I'm growing more and more nervous with each ticking minute of the kitchen clock. As the big hands on the clock keep advancing, I know this is my last chance. I pace the floor; I only need to say a few words. "You're a grandmother." That's not so hard.

I catch my breath and finally get up enough nerve. "Mom, please sit down, I have just a few words to say and I've been trying to say them all week."

This time without objection or interruption, she takes a seat at the kitchen table.

"While I lived in California, I had a daughter. You're a grandmother."

She listens thoroughly. She is with me and present for each word. She waits until I complete my entire story.

Then she says, "I'm so sorry you went through that entire experience all alone. I'm sorry you hadn't felt safe enough to tell Dad or me; we would have been there for you. I'm so sorry you were all alone."

I slowly take in her words; it's as if time had stopped. Her words calm me as she acknowledges me as her child. I hear, "They would have been there for me." This phrase heals my shame, right in that moment.

This is such a gift and I learn whatever I do, the truth can be heard. She will be there with unconditional love. My fears are unfounded.

The depth of this healing is profound and, along with heart-felt appreciation, is almost too much to take in. I experience Mom's true heart. I thought I'd come home to tell my secret for my Mom's benefit but the truth is a surprise to me. Telling my secret became a completion of this segment of my life. Telling my truth also creates an opening for sharing many more stories with my mom.

The door swings wide open and in a flash my niece and two nephews arrives on schedule for dinner. Time is moving at regular speed again; the noise level rise and fell with the excitement of dinner and everyday life.

Freedom and healing always occurs when we tell the truth. Fear and shame are released in the process.

Chapter Twelve: Acknowledging My Daughter

Returning home, I'm energized by finally telling the secret of my grown daughter. But within a week's time, a friend points out that I continue to withhold this information in everyday life.

He reminds me that when I am asked if I have any children, I typically answer, "Three stepchildren and twelve grandchildren." He notes, "You never mention you have a daughter, this seems like a secret to me."

I think about his remarks, and the next time I'm asked, I include my daughter. Then I decide to get out a picture of her at three months that the social worker sent me. I frame her picture and put it on my desk. I acknowledge her in my life.

I believe this gesture created the opening for my daughter to find me.

Within a few months of placing her black-and-white photo on my desk, the phone rings. I learn she is searching for me.

Chapter Thirteen: The Long-Awaited Call

I come home one day to a message: "We have a confidential message for you. Please call this number."

I call and leave a message in turn, asking them to please leave whatever confidential information they have on my machine since I'm the only one with access to this number. A few days later I receive a call from one of the LA area codes. They have confidential information and give me their number.

I sense this might be the long awaited call that I've prayed for; that this call is from LA County with information about my daughter.

Excited, I return the call immediately. I leave this message: "If this call is about giving permission to my birth daughter to find me, PLEASE do it now! I give you full permission to share my whereabouts my full name, address, and phone number. I request that you release all information to her now." Years before I sent a signed notarized release form to the county in case she wanted to find me. These forms were to be placed in her file to give full permission already. Still, the bureaucracy necessitates care; each step of the way is charted with releases.

A few days later the agency calls again and lets me know that my daughter has contacted the state, looking for me, and has received my name and number. They say she will contact me directly. I replay this message over and over again. My mind keeps repeating, "She's got my number. She'll call! My prayers have been answered."

A month goes by, however. I wonder if she changed her mind. I try to put her out of my mind.

Then the phone rings. I picked up to hear: "This is CD."

There is a long pause… I don't know an CD.

Then she says, "I am your daughter."

I gave her a different name. Surprise and joy combine and stumble out. I tell her I've been expecting her call.

"I'm into the Indian Way—the Native American Indian Way," she says out of the blue.

I laugh in delight; I've said those exact two phrases just like she spoke them. Our connection is made.

We talk for at least two hours and share information about our lives and our adoptive parents. Generally we find our backgrounds to be quite similar. It's quite amazing. Both our mothers are schoolteachers and our dads work, or worked, for large industry. Both our families have a strong religious foundation and a great love and gratitude for their adoptive children. This too is mind-boggling.

As we're finishing our phone conversation, CD asks, "When can we meet? How about Mother's Day?"

This goes straight into my heart. Tentatively, I ask, "When is Mother's Day?" I have no idea.

She tells me and we set up our first meeting: Mother's Day 1992. CD asks me to send a picture of myself before we met. Likewise, she sends a collection of pictures from early childhood to current day in a loving card. These snapshots throughout her life are an opening for me to gain a sense of her at different stages of her life.

Her pictures give me insight and a way to catch up and explore her childhood; I feel blessed by her thoughtfulness. In each picture I try to see the resemblance to her father and me… the color of her eyes, the shape of her face, her mouth, the way she carries herself. Until this moment I've never seen a blood relation before. In most pictures the resemblance to me and her dad are clearly there, and this is healing to see. I hope she will encounter the same even if I sent simply the only current professional picture of myself.

Chapter Fourteen: Mother's Day

My youngest sister is visiting me from Seattle at the time of CD's planned visit. We are excited, anticipating CD's arrival together as she flies in from southern California. I'm trying to remain calm but my insides are churning and my stomach is telling me just how nervous I am.

When the doorbell rings, I jump, take a deep breath and head for the door. I open it and there she is, my daughter, standing tall and vulnerable before me.

As I look at her I am in awe. We both grin. I nervously invite her in. She's wearing light blue jeans and a navy print shirt, her curly blond-streaked, shoulder-length hair touching her collar. Her oval face and smile, I think, are similar to mine. She clearly stands two inches taller than me.

I expected to run and hug her when she arrives, like you see on TV, but we both stand back at arm's length, tentative, assessing each other and sensing ways to connect. It is the first time either of us have ever seen a birth relative and someone who remotely looks like us. We stand awkwardly; I don't know how much time goes by as we stand like this, but finally I find my words and welcome her into my home and introduce her to my sister.

We all sit down and talk for a while. Then the conversation disappears and what remains is a lifetime of feelings, along with pure delight. This is a day I have longed for. In the silence it feels like we are both trying to take in each other's energy and to recognize one another at the deep level of the heart.

Sometime passes… and we walk to a small neighborhood restaurant for lunch.

Walking down the street together, my sister begins to note out loud our similarities. She comments how we walk the same, throwing out our right leg, and we both have short, crooked little fingers. Then she laughs with pleasure at her observations. She goes on pointing out other similarities: you both have skinny legs and large breasts. My own observation intensifies. I notice our sloping shoulders and how we both reach to pull up the bra straps that fall off our shoulders. It feels natural to capture these ordinary things, yet we are just now experiencing them for the first time. Over lunch we continue to discover other things, like we listen to a lot of the same music and read the same books.

Over the years we laugh when we send the same greeting cards to each other.

Our careers are similar too. In my teens I worked each summer, running a private beach club, teaching swimming lessons and life guarding. My first professional job was as the Aquatic Director for a YMCA. She loves the ocean and worked part time each summer at a Wildlife Center, explaining marine life to kids. She can be found regularly playing in the ocean, chasing after the spinnaker dolphins and waiting for the sight of whales. Her professional life is as a Recreational Therapist. And our careers have both developed into the healing arts. CD studied holistic healing and is now a Massage Therapist, weaving a blend of many modalities into her practice. My journey has unfolded as a Spiritual Healer, wherein I weave the spiritual, emotional, mental and physical realms into balance and open clients to their heart–wisdom. In the healing arts we've experienced parallel situations—and now we get to share these experiences. It's clear to me how our DNA has driven our life choices and contributes to our similarities,creating parallel spirituality. It is a blessing to know my daughter and to see our reflections.

For an adoptee to experience a blood relation is indescribable. It is a blessing. Our secrets are held in the DNA. Our souls are happy we have met and I feel a deep bond I never felt possible.

Chapter Fifteen: My Daughter's Fear

CD called one night in fear, saying she felt like a caged animal and was pacing the floor, anxious and alone. I too had this exact experience and used the same words to describe what I was feeling. She had just ended a relationship, and although she wanted the relationship to end, this is how she felt. I walked with her through her feelings and spoke to her infant child, comforting her.

From my perspective as an adoptee, I share with CD; these feelings are triggered by the loss of our birthmother's heartbeat. These feelings are what we experienced when we were separated from our heart connection with our birth mother. When our hearts connect deeply to a lover, and then we break this connection, our inner infant may feel this same loss again and reacts in a preverbal way.

Before I understood this preverbal panic, I described these feelings as dropping into the deep hole or falling into the void. Now I recognize this experience as moving into the heart wound. It is my experience when I have released my connection to a lover, I have had this grave fear of being alone, triggered by my inner infant's separation from the familiar heartbeat of my mother while in the womb. It is the inner infant's response to the loss of the birth mother's heartbeat.

I have felt this wound twice in my lifetime; so in this moment, I was able to hear CD fully and totally empathize with her. We walked through her fear together. It was satisfying to be able to be there for her and to make a difference, since I felt my absence had caused her reaction.

In my mind once more we were charting parallel life experiences—set up by parallel experiences at the beginning of our lives.

Note: This story is written from my perspective of what transpired and does not necessarily reflect my daughter's beliefs.

Chapter Sixteen: Day with Wolves

My daughter comes on one of her yearly visits and she suggests that we visit the wolf sanctuary. We both have history of loving wolves, having had them even as spirit guides. So we decide to spend one day of her trip visiting the wolves at a wolf sanctuary in New Mexico.

I am always excited when she comes to visit but I usually have feelings of anticipation, no matter how marvelous every moment is. I think this is due to my abandonment history; and her trust issues with me, which cause us to be tentative with each other.

As we head to the wolf sanctuary few words are spoken. However, within the sanctuary, CD becomes animated. She has made an appointment with a guide to actually go into the enclosures to visit certain wolves with her camera. She wants to experience them up close. One wolf, Sassy, gives her a kiss on her face and she pets her, which is quite unusual since wolves are really shy. While she visits certain wolves, I take the guided tour of the entire sanctuary and learn the stories about each wolf and why they've been rescued and how they came to live in the sanctuary. We meet up at the end of our experiences, both feeling deeply touched and blessed by the wolves. When we arrive home CD spends hours on the computer creating an incredible photo album from the amazing pictures she took. Her love is shown through these special actions.

For me the relationship with my daughter is complex, just as my relationship with my adoptive family is complex, yet the nature of these relationships is reversed. In my adoptive family there is no DNA recognition, and with my daughter we share DNA but we lack the day-to-day sharing of our history. We are lucky to have meshed in our adoptive families' history and values, which are similar and different. Our life values stem from our upbringing.

Because our past was void of each other's presence, we are tentative with each other, as if at times we are walking through a minefield testing each other. There is that murky beginning, that primal place of connection; but the foundations are a river, are liquid. How can we build on this? But the smells, the sounds, the heart beat is still there in the unconscious, waiting to be acknowledged by us both. There is love but no history of love.

There is remembered infant history of loss between us; as well as, chosen and special memories with our adopted parents. There is the question what is the relationship of birthmother and daughter? How do we come together and relate to each other? Without the day to day foundation, and early childhood bond, connecting, bonding and trusting can be an opportunity. So in our relationship there is always an edge, an undercurrent of questions: Will I show up? Can I live up to the expectations my daughter holds for me? What are those expectations?

As difficult and complex as it is, we come together—wanting our connection that was lost at birth. We realize this is important and are willing to heal it by coming together and relating as best we can.

Note: Again this story is written from my life perspective and does not necessarily reflect my daughter's view of how she holds our relationship.

Chapter Seventeen: My Mother's Death

When my mom is dying, my work keeps me from going home to visit her. Because I speak with her daily on the phone, I rationalize I am with her during her dying process. After her death, however, I feel I had abandoned her.

Two years later, I participate in a full moon sweat lodge ceremony. The leader suggests that we go back in time, seven generations, and connect with our elders. I wonder which relatives I am to connect with—I am stopped, I have no blood elders that I know. I know spirit elders and adopted elders, but where is my connection to my blood?

I sing, therefore, to whoever wants to hear me, I sing my feelings of loss. I sing to my (adoptive) mom. I sing to her of my love. I apologize to her for all the times I tested her love. I apologize to her for not being physically present with her when she died. I ask for her forgiveness. I sing thanks to her for all her love and gifts to me throughout my life. I thank her for being Mom. And I weep.

This ceremony is the healing for all the times in my life when a seminar leader would instruct the participants to look at one's family of origin, and I would feel lost and confused, wondering, *What does that mean, which family am I to look into?* Each time I felt orphaned and connected to my adopted family. No one taught me it was okay to honor both family histories. Singing to my ancestors taught me I could honor the entire me and include my adopted family in so doing. I have many relatives of love.

Chapter Eighteen: Finding Lost Parts of Me

After my mom's passing, I feel I need a break from the fast paced world of work to go deeper into my spiritual journey. I lease out my condo and find a three-month rental; my stay extends nearly two years. Mount Shasta City has a population around 2000 people. It seems just the right place to commune with myself in the quiet of nature and the energy of the mountain.

Mt. Shasta City, California, is a cauldron for change and awakening. One day in the mail, I receive an article outlining Soul Retrieval, sent by a healer friend. As I read through the article,I'm transported to some inner knowing from times past—drawn into the words as if I am entering a trance. When I finish reading, I sit in silence and let the words initiate me.

My curiosity is piqued. The article explains visiting three realms: the above world, the below world and the world in-between to retrieve fragmented parts of the soul. I decide to travel these worlds. Would I have any parts missing that I need to discover or retrieve? What would I discover in these different realms?

The article outlines the method shamans use to journey with their clients into the other worlds. The shaman drums his client into a trance state. When the client goes off to one of the worlds,the shaman accompanies him or her. Once they reach a particular world, they look for soul fragments that need retrieval. It seems so perfect.

As I read, my inner wisdom tells me I can do this. The journey may be different going by myself, but I know I can ask and be guided as I travel. I'll experiment. It seems possible because this is much how I understand the worlds we inhabit.

The above world is an ethereal realm where light spirits, angels, archangels and ascended beings hang out. The below world is the spiritual realm that is earth based. Animal spirits, fairies, mineral spirits reside in this realm. The in-between realm, I believe, is where unity of the realms comes together. I have seen this place when I call the seven directions and create a sacred circle. I have seen dancing spirits there.

It's time to begin. I align myself with the light and journey in the protection of Divine Light. My journey's purpose is to travel to the other worlds and find any part of my soul that wants to come home to me.

In preparation, I clean my space for ceremony. As a healer, I have learned that if you are going to take a spiritual journey, it is important to prepare the space where you will do the ceremony or ritual. It's critical to keep the space clear of any unwanted spirits not aligned with your purpose. I gather my tools: a large white candle that I light, white sage and abalone shell, a gifted feathered wing, and minerals for the four directions of the medicine wheel, animal ally items and other sacred items my rattles and drum. I place some white sage into the abalone shell and light it. Then, using the owl wing, I fan the flames out, leaving a trail of smoke. Once the sage is smoldering, I draw the smoke to my heart with the wing, then gently scoop the smoke up over my head and down my arms. Once I have smudged my arms, I brush the smoke down the front of my body, then hold the shell around behind my back and smudge my back from shoulders towards the ground. In the process, I ask for cleansing of my entire energy field. And I ask for guidance on my journey.

Next I offer the smoke to the six directions: up to the Creator, down to the Earth Mother, then to the North, East, South and Westerly directions. Finally I smudge my drum, crystals and all the sacred items I have gathered. I lay out on the floor a circle of stones in alignment with the four directions: North, East, South and West. I place my sacred minerals and animal allies in their aligned positions on the wheel. Once the circle is complete, I enter through the easterly direction and sit down facing north.

I am ready to create the ceremony within this sacred circle. I begin to drum by calling in my guides, the Grandmothers and Grandfathers from all the directions—North, East, South and West, the Above World and Below World and The Center of all Being. I call in my Animal Allies for each of these. Once all my spiritual guides are present, I ask for a mantle of protection around my home and me. Then I begin to embark on my journey.

I drum and ask to journey to the upper world. I drum myself into trance. As I drum, I find myself slipping into a space I can't quite explain. It looks like nothing I have ever seen. I am traveling rapidly, feet first in a horizontal position, within a slip of space. Above and below me is what looks like reddish brown-crated land-masses. The only space I can see for miles upon miles is this space between, and then I'm dumped out into the heavens filled with stars. The space twinkles brightly all around and the expanse is vast, like the dark blue black of the ocean at night. Somehow this space feels very familiar.

I breathe and take in my surroundings. I see a bright ball of light, like a star, moving towards me. As it gets closer I see it is a translucent light being holding something in its arms. This star being continues to move into closer range until I see what it holds. A baby. Then it enters my energy field, reaches out, and presses this young baby into my heart. I draw back, feeling this newness. I'm surprised and soothed at the same time. Then as quickly as I left to journey, I find myself traveling backwards until I feel myself back in my home, sitting in silence. I feel a profound shift within my body, I am vibrating at a new frequency, and I feel reorganized and fuller somehow. Wow, amazing.

I rest; an hour or so passes and I decide to journey to the below world. I wonder what I'll discover. Again I align with my guides and totems and begin to drum. This time my Horse Totem comes forward, and I climb up on his back and we journey together. My horse grows wings and we gallop and fly, depending on the terrain. Then suddenly we arrive in a grassy meadow in front of a singular large, old oak tree. I dismount. A young girl of about five peeks out from behind the tree. "Who are you?" I ask.

She replies, "I'm part of you but I got lost here. I've been waiting for a long time to be found."

"I'm sorry it took me so long to come for you. Would you like to come home with me now?"

There is the smallest of small *yes*.

With this yes, my Horse ally crosses his front legs and kneels down, inviting the young one to climb up onto his back. "Hold onto my mane, little one, hold on tight; we have a long way to travel to get home."

I somehow disappear; only the young one remains and she speeds through space, galaxies and star systems until back in my home. It's as if I merged with her and we're hanging on to the horse's mane for dear life, yet protected and safe. Then I notice that we are both home. Again I rest.

On my third journey, now to the center world, I forget to set an intention, so as I travel, I just notice the space around me and return home. I meet no one.

Over the next few weeks following this experience, I find myself a bit disoriented yet expanded. As the integration process continues, I feel more whole.

Healing

SPIRITUAL AWAKENING:
Part Four: Healing Exercises

Ex 1: Creating Sacred Space
Ex 2: Opening Your Chakras
Ex 3: Calling Guides & Helpers
Ex 4: Connecting to Your Higher Self
Ex 5: Connecting to Spirit

LEARNING ABOUT YOURSELF
Part Four: Healing Exercises

Ex 7: Mirrors
Ex 9: Art Exercises
Ex 10: Becoming One with Mother Earth
Ex 13: Using Full Body Awareness in Making Decisions

STORIES
Part Two: Journey of Triggers & Healing

Ch 11: A Journey Home to Tell the Truth
Ch 12: Acknowledging My Daughter
Ch 13: The Long-Awaited Call
Ch 14: Mother's Day
Ch 15: My Daughter's Fear

Ch 16: Day with Wolves
Ch 20: Vibrational Blocks
Ch 21: 55th Birthday
Ch 24: Longing is a Trigger to Fill Ourselves

CORE WOUNDS STORIES ▶ Part One: Abandonment - Loss - Adoption Confusion

The Void (is in the introduction of the book
   and also can be found in Part Four: Introduction)
Ch 1: The Beginning: The Primal Wound
Ch 3: What We Do to Belong-Secondary Wounds
Ch 4: Divided Self, Divided Language

Ch 2: Where Did I Come From
Ch 5: Are You My Brother?
Ch 6: The Passport Experience
   Triggers from the Past
Ch 7: Bringing It All Together

athways

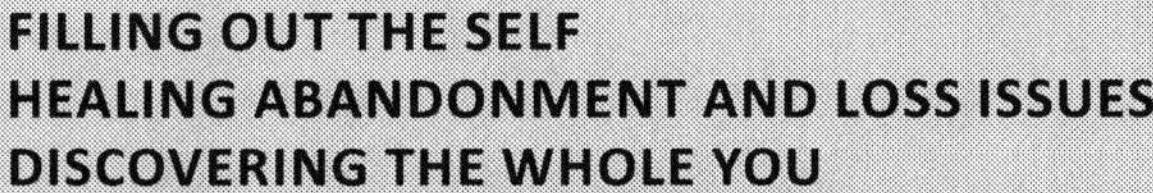

FILLING OUT THE SELF
HEALING ABANDONMENT AND LOSS ISSUES
DISCOVERING THE WHOLE YOU

STORIES

Chapter Nineteen: Connecting to my DNA: Meeting my Birth Mother and Father

Mother

One morning just after meditating, while living in Austin, I begin to experience a rash of fearful thoughts. Thoughts with fears I have never experienced before. It is odd somehow; they are situations that never frightened me before. I worry about what is happening to me.

So I call a psychic friend and ask for assistance. She says that these thoughts and fears originate from my birthmother. That she is trying to make her transition into the next world, and she doesn't want to carry these fears with her. She feels that since I am strong, I can resolve them for her.

I thank my friend for her wisdom and we hang up.

•

As a healer I call the ancestors and create sacred space. I ask my birth mother into the sacred circle so that we can talk together. I have never met or talked with my birth mom. I welcome her, and after a few minutes I let her know I have received her fears. I also let her know that I am unwilling to clear her fears for her—and furthermore it isn't my responsibility to do so. I explain she can take these thoughts with her and work on clearing them from the other side.

She was unaware this was possible, she says. I ask her to reclaim her thoughts and fears from my being, and she does so.

I tell her she can invite the angels for guidance on her journey as she handles her fears. I bless her and thank her for coming. I release her energy back to her physical self.

My emotions stabilize; I feel myself. Her thoughts and fears are no longer part of me.

Father

There is a spirit over your left shoulder. Do you know who it is?
Six months after experiencing my birth mother's fears, I visit my friend in

Dallas. As we are catching up, she says, "There is a spirit in white over your right shoulder, a woman; do you have any idea who it might be? I usually see relatives that have just passed over."

I say, "Ask her if she is my mother."

She nods affirmatively. The spirit then says, "I'd like you to talk with your brothers and make amends for me."

My answer comes from deep within. "I can't do that, I don't know them and it is for you to do anyway. You can send them messages from where you are. You can ask the angels to help you. Once again this is not my job. However, if you would like to have my brothers find me and tell me their names, that would be helpful to me."

She doesn't respond. I let her know I'm glad to know she has made her transition and I send her blessing. My friend reports she is gone.

Then she says, "There is someone else here, over your left shoulder, he is in a thousand pieces."

I'm hesitant to ask. "Is he my dad?"

"Yes."

I tell her I want to do an experiment. She agrees. I call on my guides and ask as I tone, *Can I bring my father back energetically into wholeness? Would this serve my dad?* They reply that I can and it will serve him greatly.

With that affirmation I align to my dad's energy and let a tone form within myself, with the intention of bringing all fragments of my dad together into perfect harmony. As I tone, my friend begins to see movement of particles coming together into wholeness. I tone until he is one with himself. It is incredible.

Once he is whole, my father begins to talk with me for the first time. He tells me he was killed in the war—blown apart. He thanks me for his new wholeness. He tells me he never knew about me until my mother transitioned and he is so pleased to see me and meet me. He asks if I would be willing to let him assist and guide me on my journey. He suggests that I begin to learn more about the many faces of the goddess, that it will serve me on my journey. I am blown away by his presence and the love I feel from him. He says I can call on him anytime. I say I will.

And with this knowing, we end our dialogue he goes on. I sit, stunned and excited in silence for a long time, just taking in all that transpired.

During the next conversation with my birth dad, I draw his face. He has large eyes and black long hair in a braid. He tells me his name is John, and he weaves stories of our Native American heritage. When he says he's a third generation medicine man, this affirms my knowing and profoundly touches my heart. As we speak I feel his hands wrap around me. He holds me tight to his chest, and in this embrace, I travel through time, moving through many generations alongside my ancestors back to my beginnings.

I wonder after these experiences what life would have been like if I had known him and these ancestral roots.

•

Many years later, during a chiropractic session, both my parents come to assist the chiropractor who is trying to bring healing. They work with her in my session and send messages to fill in more gaps in my knowing. They say how they were unable to wed at the time I was conceived, he being native and my mom being white. He says he is glad I was able to live in the white world, for it is easier. He tells me his medicine name is Johnny Running Wolf. This resonated within me, as the wolf has always been with me and is my main totem during my healings sessions with clients. He tells me of his love for my mom—"Dorrie," Doris. I'm touched again by their coming and how it confirms my knowing.

Chapter Twenty: Vibrational Blocks

I have learned that through our vibrations, we are like magnets, drawing people and events into our lives. In the process, our friends and relatives mirror different aspects of us. When we are conscious, we can learn from these mirrors. When we are unconscious, we continue to draw people and situations that show us our internal wounds and outside behaviors and beauty.

The following is a series of unconscious vibrations related to my preverbal infant.

A chiropractor and medical intuitive friend is visiting from Austin. Over a week's worth of conversations, we discover and reveal a pattern of "surprise physical abuse" in my history. Because this pattern was scattered over large gaps of time, I didn't see the relationship between these random acts. The perpetrators were all total strangers.

1966: I was pulled over and attacked by two police officers from a small beach town in southern California.

1967: I was forced off the freeway by two guys who tried to attack me. I kicked them and got away.

1981:In Houston, I was raped and beaten in my home by a stranger.

1993:As I was moving out of my condo, a man forced his way onto the elevator, pushing and shoving me and the movers.

1996: I was pushed to the ground, threatened and stood over by a Rental Truck Employee who came to drop off a car trailer.

These events come rolling out of my mouth. My friend and I both notice that these seemly separate events looked familiar. Through closer examination, we notice that each incident occurred within three months of a major move or life transition. That number seems to mean something. I was adopted when I was three months old.

As a chiropractor and trained to see patterns of blocked energy, my friend, Dr. KA, sees I am holding a vibration in my kidneys that draws 'surprise attack/abuse' to me.

As she checks my physical body system, she discovers the distortion/vibration held in my kidneys is linked to my feelings of abandonment (fear) when adopted

at three months old. I think I would feel **found**, being adopted. However, I experience the fear of the unknown of another new beginning. When I was born I was
taken away from the familiar heartbeat of my mother and given to strangers in the
hospital for care. At three months I was placed with my adopted family—a major
transition for a preverbal infant. Somehow this fear I experienced has gotten locked
up as a vibration in my kidneys. In my case the fear of the unknown is so great
within the infant part of me that during major life transitions, the fear vibration
gets activated and draws fear-based experiences to me.

To correct this distortion my friend adjusts my body and shifts the blocked
vibrations, allowing my kidney to come back into alignment with its normal func-
tioning. She then prescribes a twenty-five-day vegetable and fruit fast to boost my
kidneys back into balance with my overall body. After these adjustments and fast,
I no longer draw abusive experiences like a magnet into my life during times of new
beginning transitions.

Chapter Twenty-One: The 55th Birthday Message

I've invited a group of girlfriends to come to the redwoods to celebrate my birthday through a ceremony. We sit together enclosed in a grove of beautiful and fragrant redwood trees. I ask my friend Anne to call the sacred circle while the rest of us drum and rattle. Once this is called, I welcome each friend, feeling deep gratitude for them being part of my life. I am delighted to be in their presence. Then one by one my friends acknowledge me and tell me how I've touched them in their lives. I open and receive their word gifts and their love.

As we complete our sharing around the circle, Anne says out of nowhere, "Your birthmother would like to speak to you through me."

I bow my head, my heart opening.

Anne begins to channel my mother. The words flow smoothly:

"I have come to acknowledge your bravery. I was not brave like you. I have been watching as you have accomplished many things. I am very proud of you. I never wanted you. I tried not to connect with you in the womb. I had my own life. I'm sorry."

After a moment, I reply:

"I understand. I, too, have a daughter I gave up for adoption. It's okay. I believe we chose our parents and our journey. Thank you for carrying me into this world. My heart has always loved your heart. I have missed you all of my life, but I realize my primal wound is my soul's journey."

She answers, "You are much braver and smarter than I am. Your journey is much bigger. I don't really understand this soul stuff, but I honor you, my daughter. Happy Birthday."

In turn, I say, "Thanks so much for coming. Thank you for your blessings."

She is gone.

My surprise runs deep.

We go on with the ceremony, and when we are finished, we thank the ancestors and guides who have come. We close the sacred circle and head back to my house to change and get ready for dinner.

Later, at my boyfriend's home, I share how my birth mother came into the sacred circle celebration. In the middle of telling the story, I burst into tears and sobs, only broken by: "I wish I had known my mom, I wish I had met her just once."

He wraps his big arms around me and holds me while I cry. And then, like the tears broke loose and dropped away, I feel complete. Holding me was exactly what my little girl and I needed; I was able to mourn and be held with love at the same time. This holding was a perfect healing moment in acknowledging the loss of my mother.

Chapter Twenty-Two: Taking a New Name

I have a birth name hidden from me; I have an adoptive name I never felt connected to. I have a married name, which was anchored in a new family's role for me. After my divorce I feel like this name is not me anymore. So it is time to find a new name just for me.

Liz Ashling is my new name, I chose it. I am beginning to realize that within each chapter of disappointment, frustration and disconnection, there is within me an equal healing experience—a completion of one cycle unfolding into another. These cycles have not always been conscious, but rather, they push up and out of me like a seedling pushes the soil away to break free of the topsoil and be in direct contact with the sun. It is from this germinating place, for five years now, that I have yearned for a new name.

Liz Ashling was birthed in stages. First I shared my desire to find a new name with a client from Ireland, and after some time she suggested the name Ashling, a Celtic name meaning dreaming. I liked it. It felt right. Ashling represents the healer who takes people into sacred space it is a form of dreaming, a way of working in a dream state. Cool. Then as I thought more, I realized how I want to live from a place of grace and how the work I do helps people weave their stories back into wholeness. Out of that thought process, I played with the name, Grace Ashling Weaver. However I realized I did not want to be called simply by Grace, so I waited for more insight.

Interestingly, at this time my boyfriend said my name didn't fit me, so he called me *dearest*, creating a safe space for me to inhabit as I waited for the correct name to show itself.

One evening I was sharing a little about myself with a client during a week-long retreat. We were talking about aging. I made a comment about feeling old and frumpy. She laughed and said, *You have a beauty like Liz Taylor—you glow and your eyes are so deep they shine with light*, and she laughed. From that moment of sharing, she began to call me Liz and Elizabeth. I loved it, Liz felt fun and light.

After I had chosen Liz as my name I remembered my adopted mom's name was Elizabeth, though she always went by Betty. Claiming the name Liz honored my adopted mom as well as me.

The following week I decided to test out the name Liz Ashling. I sat in front of a full-length mirror, in the quiet of my bedroom, and slowly said each of my names:

Cherlye Anne L. (my birth name),

Martha Jane K.(my adopted name),

Marty D. (my married name).

With each name I noticed the energy within me. Did I look alive with these names? Not anymore. Then I said, *Liz Ashling*, and I saw a new lightness, a deep calmness and a child's delightful smile. I had found my new name. It felt right.

I called my boyfriend with my new name; he loved it and began calling me Liz right away. I told my girlfriends, they all supported my new name too. It seemed no matter whom I told, there was no resistance, and no why do you want to do that, just, "You will have to give me time to adjust, to get use to your new name." Everyone, including family, heard and acknowledged my name change. My sister said, "I'll put you in the A's of my phone book right now."

The energy seemed to build around my name change, I felt completely supported in taking this name.

In December 1999, I wrote a name change announcement to clients and friends. I mailed them with my Christmas cards. By the New Year, I was on my way to stepping fully into my new name.

It wasn't until the last of the announcements had been mailed that I began to wonder what my new name meant. From a Divination book I researched the numeric combinations of letters, and then using the tarot numbers and definitions to define my new chosen name. My numerical vibration aligned with The Healer. I was surprised and delighted. I called my daughter and asked her to look in her Celtic Tree resource book for the meaning of the ash tree. She told me that the ash is the deepest rooted tree in the world.

I had always wanted roots. My heart sang to this awareness.

Ling means small, so I am a small ash tree unfolding into new life. The ash tree in the Celtic tradition is also aligned to the Ruins, an ancient oracle tradition helping people move from confusion to awareness and then to fulfillment. This Celtic information is aligned to my business practices. I use these stages in doing transformational and healing work.

I was blown away by the synchronicity and by the deepening discoveries.

I had some physical reactions to my new name. I developed a cough and my lungs were full. Under my left arm I noticed a large red mark, which looked like a birthmark in the shape of a star. I called for assistance with my lung condition and was told I was purging my previous lives connected with my previous names. I was opening space within me to realize the new me. This vibration of this new name was spinning out the old. The birthmark lasted under my left arm until the cough was cleared. Then under my right arm there appeared another red mark shaped like a five-pointed star. It lasted until my name was legalized through the courts and then it faded away.

With each step in the process of my name change—registering the papers with the courts—publicizing the new name—setting the court date—notifying and changing all my legal documents from one name to the other—celebrating with my clients who gave me my new names—I felt a subtle ripple within my system, a new verification of who I am at core and who I am becoming out in the world.

On my birthday in 2000, nine months after I sent out my new name announcements to clients and friends, I birthed my name into the world.

Chapter Twenty-Three: An Infant Self

A break-up with another boyfriend triggers night terrors and discovery of an infant self.

It is Thursday morning and I'm running late. I have to stop for gas and must make it to the city. The traffic is intense, with an accident pulled over to the side of the freeway entrance. I am forced to sit at the end of my street, waiting. I pray for perfect timing, I need to make my massage appointment. I've just ended a relationship with the man of my dreams and I really need to be touched and soothed. The end of this relationship has triggered the terror again. In stepping away I now feel trapped in myself.

I spent Tuesday night wrestling with myself. Finally I went to bed at 1:30 a.m. after cleaning, straightening, busying myself to put off the inevitable trying to sleep. I lay down only to pop up again and again, to be jarred out of sleep, feeling "empty." I forced myself into this empty place and sobbed, but afterward the tension built and I felt more terror. I sat up and turn on the light, figuring I had another late night ahead. I reached for my yellow pad and pen to write anything and everything that is disturbing me. If only I can get to the why this is happening, why the sleeplessness. I hadn't experienced anything like this since a boyfriend left unexpectedly fourteen years previous.

I know about these emotions. I work with people and their terror. I've checked my entire system to see how my inner children are; I have reassured them that this move to separate is good and right. I am here and we are supported by many friends and surrounded by all the spiritual guides and angels. Even in the mist of these feelings of knowing, the terror persists. I need to sleep but I am wide awake and full of energy and determination not to sleep. I can't lie down because the pain seems too great. I must distance myself and figure this out. I meditate and come into calmness. I lay down to rest now, I look over at the clock, and it is 5:00 am, no, no sleep yet I am awake again, 15 minutes has passed. I get up and write some more. 7:00 a.m. It's light now. I lie down and sleep for an hour and a half and I'm up again. I haven't been able to find any parts of myself who feel abandoned or alone.

I make it to my appointment, only fifteen minutes late. I rush up the stairs and into the massage room. I quickly undress and climb up on the massage table to lie down, but before I put my head down, I pop up and say, "I just don't want to lie down, I feel so sad when I lie down. I've got to let go of this relationship fully, I've got to stop this fight within me."

Deb places her hands between my shoulder blades and down over the back of my heart center. "I take it you'd like just a loving, nurturing massage today."

I shake my head and lie face down on the table.

Deb and I go back along way. We first met in a dance class and I have been coming to her for massage and healing for twelve years now. As she works, she speaks softly of what she picks up within my body. Today, there is no new information. Then once again she pauses over my heart center. "Oh, oh, there is a very small baby here, very small, **4 days** old."

When she says this, words keep rushing out, "She's afraid she will always be alone and feel *empty.*"

There it is—the meaning of the word empty, the deep feeling of loss. My four-day-old lost her mother's heartbeat; she's in the hospital all alone without her mom's rhythm, empty, so "empty."

Deb encourages me to go into "empty"; I feel the loss of my mother. I realize in opening my heart fully to Jack and feeling his heart sweetness, it had filled the void in my heart, the void left by the loss of my birthmother. I weep knowing this truth. With this realization, I release my feelings of terror through my flowing tears. I am free. I feel great. I still feel deep love for Jack, but I am freed by this new knowing, unattached to our journey's outcome. I realize our relationship will unfold as it is meant to.

Acknowledging Deb's support, I once again appreciate the importance of having ongoing support to call on when things grab a hold of us, and we can't explain what is happening or when a situation is too scary to go into it alone.

My four-day-old feels safe in the sweetness of our blended heartbeats. Being conscious can't always surface our deep-seeded wounds. If this relationship had not come to an end, this four-day-old probably would have gone undiscovered, living happily in the rhythm of his heart, feeling no threat. It was not until he needed time with himself that terror was triggered. Within the safety of love and intimacy, our biggest fears can surface for us to heal. This ending is one more gift, one more piece of my heart-wound healed. I am reminded again that the only way to heal is to go into the fear or pain. The way out is through. As I begin to move back into myself and integrate this new knowing, I am free from fear and ready to approach love without attachments.

I believe we are given the experiences we need to evolve. Being in this relationship is a true gift into heart sweetness, intimacy and love. My human journey continues.

Chapter Twenty-Four: Longing is only a trigger to fill ourselves

For four months, I have been doing new work, Bodynamics, to help heal my infant children from ages three months within the womb to twelve years. This work reprograms the muscles, talking to them, giving them the messages they missed during early childhood development. This new work is healing me. After four months, I have returned to waking with a full heart, my body is gaining structural strength, becoming a place to hold me, to cradle me naturally. I am learning more about holding onto my boundaries, about coming from within my total self when I reach out or open to others. The new awareness has created a sense of inner safety. The work has brought me in touch with my mystery, my strengths and my weaknesses. I have learned through this new work that my weaknesses don't have to run me; I can nurture them, grow them and heal them. This work of touch and new understanding of cell and muscle development is available to heal the raw, abandoned, preverbal parts of anyone who has early childhood trauma. I have stepped in.

PART THREE

Sacred Psychology - Spiritual Foundation

Experiences that shape our core knowing

As I look back on my life, I see how I was tuned into my spiritual life from a very young age. I explored my environment for clues in how to be in the world, and in so doing, my personal persona developed in parallel with my unconscious spirituality. I had an innate desire for certain expressions of self. I grabbed onto certain activities that aligned with my heart's truth and spun these vibrations all around me. These earlier experiences resided securely into my memory for future use.

In these memories I see now how my spirit developed in unconscious ways, keeping me true to my innate nature. Being in and near **water** was essential to my well-being. Listening, singing and dancing to all kinds of **music** touched and enriched my heart and enlivened my whole being. Two additional events seeded my later journey: attending a Billy Graham revival when seven with my dad and always choosing to be a Native American when playing games with friends. These experiences grew my spirit until other events in my life brought me further into consciousness.

This section is about finding those vibrations in all our lives.

Chapter Twenty-Five: Water

In the summers our family headed to our cottage for two to three weeks. The cottage sat on the east side of T-Lake, a small inland lake near Lewiston, Michigan. The log cabin was situated among the quiet of big pines and ferns covering the sandy ground. This particular year of my memory, I am four and Dad and I walk down the weaving path for my first swimming lesson. There, off a small wooden dock, he gently lowers me into the clear green tinted water, silky to the touch, and

I stretch out my small lean body. I lie on the surface, moving my arms and kicking my legs as Dad holds me in his large, warm arms.

Swimming feels natural; I immediately know what to do. I feel no fear. I feel pure pleasure being in the water, moving. Dad takes me three feet from the dock and positions me to paddle back—then with a push, he lets go. I catch my own momentum and swim all the way to the dock.

He shows me how to take a big breath and hold it, to put my face right down in the water and look around. I try it, it's fun. With my eyes wide opened, I can see the bottom covered with beautiful rocks and what looks like a miniature forest of bright green trees. I raise my head and breath and sink my head under the surface again. Into the cool smooth water I go, drinking in the deep quiet below the surface.

In delight I spend hours playing in the water, discovering all the ways to glide effortlessly on the surface. As I get older I graduate to swimming across the lake, Dad in the rowboat, following along next to me.

I have loved the water ever since. It is a place for me to be with myself without distractions. The moment I dive into its quiet, I am with me and the water, skimming the surface, breathing in and breathing out, shutting out the outside world, coming into full contact with myself, in touch with my heart and my spirit.

One summer in my early teens, I stayed at Lake Huron with a neighborhood family as a nanny. The cottage sat right on the expansive white sand beach. Every afternoon while my two young charges napped, I spent hours floating in the cool expansive lake, making up water ballet routines and dreaming my future into being.

Later as a teenager, I worked as a lifeguard and taught swimming lessons at a local beach club located on a near-by inland lake. I learned to water-ski and to lean way out to catch the ski rudder's spray. I delighted in jumping the wake, pulling in the rope slack, to turn and crisscross the wake again and again until my legs turned to rubber and I gave the signal to return to shore. God, it's exhilarating. I've come to realize, no matter the water activity—sailing, rowing, skiing, fishing, cruising, sitting beside a rushing river, walking along the beach, or simply staring out to sea and listening to the sea as it laps the shore—when I'm there, it's all that matters. Being on or in the water, even in the bath, my lips stretch into a large grin. My heart is happy.

Along my healing journey I experienced Watsu—water massage. I step down into the warm pool, the water temperature kept equal to the body at 98.6 degrees. Submerging into the pool brings on an automatic semi-relaxed state, a place of sensing. I feel wrapped and protected in warm water nectar. As the watsu process begins, I find myself gently pulled into a cradled position, my head comfortably resting on the arm of the watsu practitioner, my lower back supported by her other arm. My body floats suspended in the water. I take in a big breath, and as I release it, I sink into my practitioners care, surrendering to her and the water. I close my eyes and feel myself being gently floated, rocked and moved slowly through the water.

As my body is moved, the warm water washes over me in a rhythmic pattern somehow akin to my own. At times, it is as if I am in the womb. I sense my own heart center and this, with the sound of the water all around me, nurtures my physical body and my soul. Watsu puts me in a deep healing trance filled with love and nurturing. When the watsu is complete, I stay sitting in the water, in a gentle trance state for an hour or so, atone with my inner rhythm.

Watsu is not readily available, so when I to want relax fully and replenish myself; I head for a bath in my home. I use the bath to detox my system after an intense day, strenuous exercise, or emotional clearing. Each time the bath allows me to re-integrate and come back into balance with myself. In the winter on cold mornings, I do my meditations in the bath and open my system by toning each chakra, and then I shower off and am balanced and ready for my day.

Water is my medium to relax, to be quiet, to release stress, to luxuriate. It assists me in coming back to myself. Water assists in shutting out the outside world so I can listen more fully to myself. Enjoying a lake or stream cleanses my body and replenishes my soul/spirit. It encourages totally surrender. Any troubles are washed away and I become calm and feel great joy. In its warm embrace, I feel I have entered into a magical place where I'm comforted and find inner peace.

Water is multi-dimensional. In all the ways water serves me, I discover its massiveness. As a symbol representing the subconscious, it also holds an unending quality. I can continually dive in and there is always more richness to discover. Water has always been a friend with which I can connect whenever I'm heading into the unknown. I enter the uncertainty through water and feel safe and reassured.

Chapter Twenty-Six: Billy Graham

I sat straight in my chair, my full attention on the front of the tent, waiting to see what comes next. I sensed the energy build, my excitement hardly contained as Billy Graham walked to the center of the stage. I listened to his strong voice and felt his compassion and heart—it seemed to come right into me.

Then there was an invitation to go down to the front of the tent, to the altar, and pledge our life to Jesus and be saved. I turned to Dad and asked if I can go; he nodded an okay. In my memory, I got in line, my dad a bit behind me, supporting me but letting me do it myself. I actually shook Billy Graham's hand and pledged my devotion to Jesus. The truth I experienced, however, was captured best in the details of the light around him, the sense of angles radiating into space—it was beyond the man himself.

I was ecstatic for weeks. I felt connected to the greater knowing from this time forward. This knowing comforted me throughout my life.

The divine touched me that day—I was expanded into a new knowing. It was an internal experience that I couldn't explain; I just knew something touched me. I was only seven but I knew God.

The experience also brought me closer to my father, allowing me to share closely in his spirituality and to gather a glimpse of my own. Later I realized that this moment awakened my soul's journey and my sense of oneness with the Divine power.

Chapter Twenty-Seven: Play at Being an Indian child

From the time I was young, I loved the wisdom the Native Americans held sacred.

I loved to play in the neighborhood bushes, finding earthly treasures to share. I wanted a leather dress and moccasins and pretty blue turquoise jewelry. On our summer trips to our cottage in T-Lake, Michigan, we stopped at the trading post and bought Indian trinkets and new leather moccasins. Thirty years later I learn why the Native People meant so much to me—it's in my DNA.

The real wisdom was paying attention to what attracted me. All it takes is staying true to our own deeper connections.

Chapter Twenty-Eight: Dance: A Soul Experience

My soul dances me. The music moves me.

When I dance, I feel connected to earth and spirit. Dance is an expression of passion from the soul.

After seeing Stomp, a dance company using garbage cans, large plastic barrels, brooms, and other everyday items to create music and dance, I joined a dozen strangers on the streets in San Francisco and danced from the theatre to the parking garage.

Two months later I watched the American Indian Dance Theater, where dancers from tribes across the country danced spirit onto the stage. I felt transported through time as I witnessed their invocation from the edge of my seat, my soul remembering the dance and the drum beat.

These experiences brought to light the way we all acknowledge truth and can move together. The importance of all our individual gifts of art is our soul's connections through time and space. We are lifted by art in all forms. Art is our conscious construction of our spiritual selves on earth.

Chapter Twenty-Nine: Music: A Precursor to Change

Music is a precursor to change; it awakens the spiral movement to new knowing.
Music is a portal to change; it is a manifestation of spirit.

I took singing lessons for five years. I dreamed of being a rock and roll singer. I studied show and pop tunes. During this time my voice came into its own resonance. When I could place my voice and really sing, I transcended my sense of self. I experienced no awareness of time. The music and the lyrics captured me fully. An hour or two of singing seemed like fifteen minutes. Once I spent an afternoon singing with a friend who has a beautiful grand piano and large collection of song books. I sang and he played song after song, for five hours. We rested and began again, it was a musical marathon.

I didn't know it then, but I was developing my voice as a vibrational healer. Now frequently I use my voice to create a particular tone to assist in opening, clearing and balancing client's different energy bodies. I have found I can use tones to assist in opening blocked chakras or emotional and physical blocks found anywhere in the body. Sounding/toning is a gentle way to enter its physicality and its secret spaces and to help energy flow more easily. It can create physical and emotional harmony. When I have a block or physical pain, I quite often put one hand or finger on the pain and tone into it until it releases.

Chapter Thirty: Stories from my Spirit Journey

1.

I embrace all types of ritual and stimuli on my spiritual journey, from earth ritual to yoga, from meditation to music, drums and rattles, and all forms of art.

It's the mid-eighties; a lot is going on in my life. I've just opened my own business, doing Human Resource Development Consulting and Training. There are some things that just keep breaking down in my marriage and I am still healing from being raped. I enroll in a six-week self-awareness class with the intention of finding my own voice, my truth, and of restoring my power. I'm looking for some sort of clarity, and a sense of where I go from here.

In this process I begin to hang out at my friend Beth's family therapy center. At this time, there is an explosion of new age practitioners coming into Houston, bringing a cornucopia of awakening programs.

My friend invites these new gurus to her center. They come and we (a small group of twelve) get to experience everyone first hand. A couple teaches us how to use quartz crystals for healing and meditation. We take Therapeutic Touch. It's exhilarating.

Jean Houston comes to Houston to speak at the opening of a women's Psychiatric Hospital and we are all invited to the opening. During Jean's speech she cautions the doctors about labeling patients. She suggests that the doctors, when treating their patients, need to stay aware and honor the whole person's journey, not to see and label them where they are at that particular moment of treatment. She points out that whenever we see someone, that person is just stuck somewhere in that process. It is not who they are. This profound message takes me weeks to fully integrate.

Some of my friends begin to lead groups in The Course in Miracles. Marianne Williamson is stepping into this part of her journey around this time. We attend a variety of workshops, meditations and alternative healing courses at Unity Church. They sponsor Shakti Guain, as well as a couple who teach financial abundance and well-being. We are all reading Shirley MacLaine's book *Out on a Limb* and Louise Hays's *You Can Heal Your Life*. When I first read Shirley's books I thought they were so far out,but then about five years into my spiritual journey, I picked up her latest book and realized I was saying some of the same things. That freaked me out and delighted me at the same time.

Our group of twelve hires a couple to lead us in a fire walk. We create the fire walk together. We put together a psychic fair, and hundreds of people come. We are trying it all and each experience opens us more. It is truly an exciting time.

During this time I am working in corporate America. My clients are conservative companies. Beth keeps telling me women need to learn how to achieve higher-level positions, start their own companies, and become more of who they are. She suggests I develop a course for woman. Within the year I create The Empowerment Course and teach it weekly, over a month's time. The course is made up of a series of guided meditations (in this, I am guided by an ancient Chinese Master FuEng; he taught me how to slow my voice into a rhythmic lower trance-like voice when I lead meditations). The course presents questions that take individuals inside themselves so that they discover who they are from the inside out. I teach them how to connect to their chakras, their personal energy centers, and to run their 'chi,' their energy, more effectively. The course introduces an awareness of spirit and teaches how to move through old patterns and stuck areas. It is a powerful course; people transform themselves and their lives.

At the end of one of these classes one of my clients hands me Lynn Andrews's first book, *Medicine Woman*: "I think you will find this book interesting." I read every one of her books as soon as they were released. They follow her spiritual journey with two Canadian Indian Shamans who support her through her struggles to find her personal power. Her journey leads her into a journey with the Sisterhood of Shields and as a writer and seminar leader. Her medicine journey synergistically parallels my internal dreaming. I can't wait for each new book to come out.

I meet Lynn Andrews at a book signing in Austin, Texas. She asks a question of the audience, I comment. She asks to speak to me at the book-signing table. It's as if we know each other from another time. In a few brief minutes I feel deeply seen and acknowledged for who I am and our collective journey.

During the time I run the empowerment classes, I also begin to see people individually. I work with people in guided meditations, awakening them to inner sight, introducing them to their higher self, grounding and centering them in their physical bodies so they could use this new expanded awareness. When asked, I begin to teach them how to use crystals. I provide them with resources about herbs and how to work with minerals. At this particular time I begin to see inside people. Sometimes when we enter mediation, I see pictures of a particular situation they ask about. Once I saw a brick wall over someone's heart, things like that.

A few years later at a professional conference on Organizational Transformation, I attend a workshop where I'm partnered with a man to do an exercise. We're led into a meditation and then asked to feel into the person in front of us and to notice if there is something there to be released. Then we are instructed to ask how the release should take place. When finished, we're to report our findings to our partner.

My partner sits in front of me in a perfect upright lotus position, legs crossed, and straight back. But when I feel into him, he's bent over completely in extreme sadness. I coax out the words, "release through center", which mean absolutely nothing to me. I report my findings and he begins to sob. I learned later he was working on releasing the pain of his ex-wife leaving him; it was very difficult for him. He is an Aikido teacher and releasing through center was a natural release point for him. I was truly amazed.

All of these experiences, the Chinese guide teaching me meditation skills, seeing the brick wall around my client's heart, and experiencing the insight in working with this man at the OT Conference, were beginnings, introducing me to what now is a long relationship with other dimensional reality, the unknown, and Great Mystery. Many experiences have brought me into relationship with Dreamtime and the Invisible world. My relationship with the sacred takes me into the ancient knowing—and all that I have learned and been before. The sacred is the teacher that births us into a new ways of being as we progress through life.

2. Using Drawing to see energy and the healing path

Drawing energy patterns gives me insights into what is happening within me and in my relationships. Having a visual picture of energy flow helps make sense of the things I'm grappling with. I draw what I feel and sense and ask questions later.

One particular day I had worked with a client, after which I had run Christ healing energy through my system for hours. When I was done working, I had trouble getting grounded and back into my centered self. I took out a drawing pad and colored pencils and began to draw pictures of the energy flows I felt. Then I drew what I was feeling as I tried to come back to myself. Later, after resting, I drew the energy in resting state. It was eye opening for me to see this transition. It brought a new understanding to me just how much energy I ran and what it took to come back into a resting state of balance.

I have clients draw; it is a way for clients to see what moves or is stuck within them, in present time. It gives us a visual construct to talk about what is going on

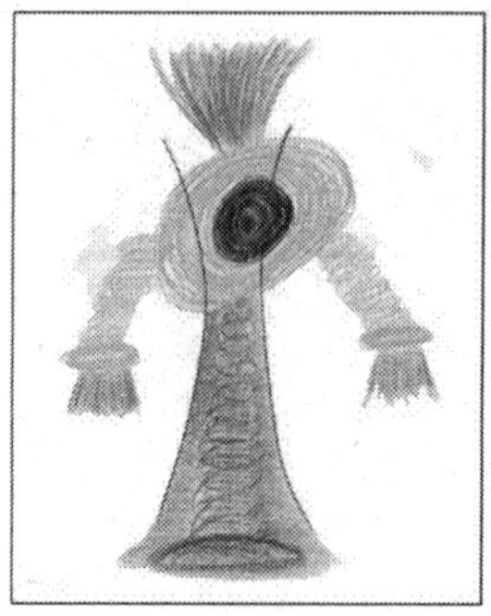 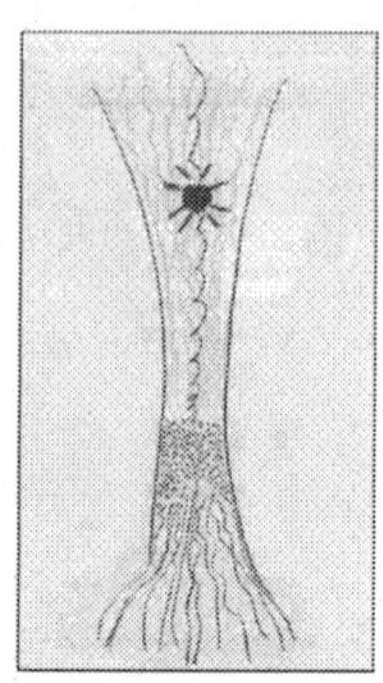

and helps them clarify situations. Drawing assists individuals to enter their subconscious and surface and to see where they are in a given moment. The process assists us in surfacing the invisible, giving sight to feelings and emotions, old trauma and stuck places. Sometimes drawing transforms emotions and trauma into what's possible. Drawing can be a powerful tool in discovering yourself and healing past wounds.

3. Realizations

It is not our adoptive parents' fault we are adopted and have our heart wound, but it is important that adoptive parents recognize their adoptive child's heart wound.

It is not our birthmother's fault we are not kept by her and given away—this is our collective wound and our joint karma. Our soul has chosen this journey to evolve in some way.

As adoptees, it is through this wound that we find our true selves, our inner power and our soul's journey.

Healing the wound of abandonment and loss is a life journey—adoption is one of the blessings along the way.

4. Physical pain tied to other dimensional healing

This is a story of the invisible energy of my birthfather, a boyfriend, my right arm and shoulder, and my inner children wanting sweetness. Bizarre as it might seem, there is a relationship between all these elements.

One sunny afternoon in August, I'm driving to a local sushi restaurant for lunch with a girlfriend. I am meandering down a side street filled with medical office buildings and a woman drives towards us, turning into me. I pull my steering wheel hard to the right in an effort to avoid a collision. At the last moment before impact, she slams on her brakes and stops, two inches short of my left front fender of my new car.

I'm shaken yet relieved. My right shoulder, however, is streaked with stabbing pain; I must have torqued it as I gripped the steering wheel. I am frozen in place, but the other car pulls behind me into the parking lot. I look around and in a flash she is gone. Slowly I pull away from the curb where I have been sitting and drive toward the restaurant. I'm still a bit shaky, my right shoulder in pain. My friend lovingly begins to rub my shoulder and upper arm, bringing me some relief. This begins an eight-month healing cycle.

After months of chiropractic, massage, Rolfing, myofascial unwinding therapy, and therapy I am still in pain. I learned that these muscles relate to some preverbal muscle groups that are under-developed in my physical body. They are related to my lack of parental bonding and my fear of abandonment. My torqued shoulder involves a weak area in my body longing to be healed. This area already carried these preverbal stories waiting to be heard.

As I heal bit by bit, I keep discovering incomplete structures that need building within my system. Revealed to me is a level of complexity of woven stories and be-liefs I would not have thought possible. Over seven months I released small pains from different muscle groups, each holding a different facet of my early childhood story. As I allow the pain and work with it, new insight is brought to the surface.

Along the way, I learn additional needs of my preverbal infants. Other older parts of me holding in the muscle groups in and around my right shoulder also appear. I learn that my young children inside want to be held, to be heard and feel secure, so I actively engage in re-parenting myself and "mothering myself well." What I uncovered is not surprising, but it is deeply informative: it is important for me to know my birthfather's love and that he honors my sweetness and me. It is important for me to honor my own sweetness and listen to myself, including the smallest and youngest of voices. It's important that I create security for myself by connecting with my divine self and introducing my inner children to this wisdom, love and divine source.

In the midst of this process, I decide to find a way to get to know my birthfa-ther. I get out my drawing pad, and on the top of a blank sheet I write, "Dad who are you—show yourself to me." I go into a semi-trance state and invite my birth father from the spiritual realm. With colored pencils in hand I draw his image. My right hand moves easily across the drawing paper and within a few minutes I have this grand portrait looking back at me: a young man's face, oval and full with high cheek bones and deep violet/blue eyes that sparkle light of yellow and green energy. His dark brown-black hair practically covering his forehead is tucked behind his ears and appears to fall loose behind him. His mouth is broad and straight across his face. His neck is long and strong. I can see his yellow and green aura around his head. I stare into this face and I begin to listen. Words begin to flow from my hand. I begin writing on the right side of the page:

"When I died I was a young man twenty. I fell in love with your mother and went off to war. I was not her husband. I had many hopes and dreams for the future. You, my dear, were a dream of mine and I'm so glad you were born. As I told you when we met, I didn't know about you until your Mother died and I am so glad you were born of so much love. You know the native way because I am part Native American—no, you are not making this up. This is why you love the songs and know the way—it is the only path for you. This is why Natives know you with honor."

I completed this writing at the bottom of the right corner on my paper. I sat with this information for quite a while, tears streaming down my face, heart touched from these words and this face staring from the page at me. I breathed in all that I had just written.

More information seemed to be coming. I began to write in the center of the page, but before the words could come, I drew an image of a red heart with arms wrapped around it and yellow light, like flames burning out its top. Then the words came again:

"Little ones, I want you to know I love you all—every one of you with all my heart and soul. I am sorry I'm not in the physical to hold you to my heart."

I stop writing again and tears of joy flow out of me in big sobs. I sit in amazement at the words and the image of the heart. All the younger parts of me seem to sigh, in delight.

After some time I pick up my pen again and in the far left column I write more:

"I am proud of you, my relative, you bring much beauty and truth to the earth at this time. You have been listening well, my daughter, listening well. You are a wise woman because you sit and listen and open your sweet heart. I am proud of you, my daughter, proud of you. Aho!"

It takes months to let in all this information from my birthfather. Parts of me question my Native American heritage, but I'm told by all my guides that this is the truth. So I honor his messages to me. I am grateful for his image.

My arm fluctuates in pain. Some days my right arm feels pinned down from the inside muscles under my upper arm and inside my armpit. When I try to reach out, I get a catching sensation like I have a knotted cuff around my upper arm. Sometimes I can work out the knots, rub and sound along my shoulder and get relief other time nothing happens. The pain is immobilizing. I begin each day taking a hot bath for flexibility. I use arnica gel on my shoulder, arm and neck, and have to resort to taking Advil regularly.

Then in my next few visits to the chiropractor, the stories under the pain become clear. Part of the pain is not even mine; it is pain from my birthfather. My arm is stuffed full of his anger and disappointments. With the chiropractor's help, we clear this pain from my body. I speak to my father and tell him it is not okay for him to use me as a vehicle for his pain—that he can clear his pain by himself from the other side. When he removes his energy, my arm and shoulder have a good deal more flexibility and I experience far less pain.

At the chiropractor's, I learn my heart and pancreas need boosting. They are depleted by deep feelings of loss. Even though I have now met my birthfather, my body and younger parts of me want him in the physical. I want to touch him in the flesh, I want to be loved, and held by him in the physical. I realize also that part of the profound loss I feel is the loss of my last boyfriend; he held me well. We cuddled for hours, holding each other. I felt financially secure and heart-connected with him. There is some interwoven feeling of loss between my birthfather and my last boyfriend. I do a clearing to release these distortions.

Each time I discover another element of unfinished past history, my arm opens, unwinds more. The throbbing pain is gone now. When I stretch/reach past my flexibility, I feel pain, but the deeper pain that inhibits walking and sleeping is gone.

The overall lesson in my right arm is, learning to be patience, allowing things to surface in their own time. The overall theme for me is to learn to let go of my own struggles. Let go of outcomes, of ideas, and people. Know my life is full when it seems empty, when I feel the loss of friends moving to different places, relationships ending—to let go and step into the void of not knowing, looking forward to what's next. Be open to receive whatever comes my way. When I let go and call the angels and archangels for support, let go and let God, I open freely.

Eight months have gone by; my arm almost has free movement. Learning to let go is an ongoing process.

Chapter Thirty-One: Four Short Healing Stories:

Fear of Being Alone

It's 1993 and I've rented an old A-frame cottage, off the beaten track, in a fairly sparsely populated area of Mt. Shasta City, California. It is just me and my dog Lady and some local deer that come visiting each day. No TV, just me with me.

I wake in fear—a bone-chilling fear of being alone. Lady, my faithful dog, is downstairs sleeping by the front door, but I feel alone. I get up and turn on the lights, walk around a bit, boil water for chamomile tea to soothe myself. I meditate some and return to bed. Within an hour I wake again in fear of being alone. In that moment, I decide once and for all I'm going to face this fear, now.

This time, as I lie in bed, I allow myself to go into the fear of being alone. I ask to feel it fully. I find the places in my body where the fear is most intense, from my throat to my stomach, and I focus my attention there. As I do I feel myself spiral down into a dark abyss. I feel surrounded in darkness, I can see nothing. I stay there in the darkness, feeling into it, the fear lessening as I face it. Then I begin to notice particles of light, and the darkness begins to break up and disperse, leaving me entirely. I find myself surrounded in a sweet calm energy. I notice this and smile, and drift off to sleep.

I have never again awakened in fear of being alone.

Stories in the belly

All the life information I didn't particularly want seemed to come into my body and get stuck there somehow. It was as if I had no control or filter to keep other people's opinions out. Later I would find myself repeating what I had heard verbatim, even when I didn't agree with what I was saying or know if it were even true. I simply repeated it as it had been said, as if it were the truth coming from me. Sometimes I judged others because of second-hand stories someone else told. I didn't even allow myself to experience my own truth in these cases. Sometimes I acted out the story within, watching myself do things I didn't want to do, but felt I had no control over and wonder why.

Recently in the midst of taking in one of these (story) suggestions, I realized

I didn't want this information in my body, but it had come in. I took a salt bath to release the anxiety of it. Then I called my therapist and told her what had just occurred and asked if she could give me any insight.

She called back with this explanation:

"When you were in the womb, you had to take in good and bad messages from your birthmother along with your food. You needed to be open to receive food. There was no filtering system from her other messages of shame, of not wanting you. Since you were abandoned, you never learned to close your umbilicus. It is still open taking in all messages. You have no filtering system. You are holding this information in your belly."

This made so much sense that I scanned back over my life. I could pull up situations where I felt controlled, almost driven to live out what others had said to me. I was trying to get the messages out of my belly. I realized if I didn't speak them, I acted them out.

Once again it was time to move through this old way of being. I prepared sacred space and, as the healer I am, asked all the stories still in my belly and not belonging to me to surface and flow out of me like a running river. I felt a strong current of energy like a swift river wash through my belly and onto the ground. When the river flow dried up, I rubbed my belly in circular motion and visualized filling it with green light, bringing the cells back into balance and memory clear of stories.

Then I sealed off the umbilicus imagining a weaving of golden light, sounding a tone to bring the weaving into being over my belly button and belly.

Journey into the Earth Mother for healing

I wanted some motherly attention and love. My adoptive mother had died. I decided I would call on the Earth Mother for comfort and refuge. I closed my eyes and began to journey asking to know the Earth Mother as my mother. I asked to be held by her and to know/feel her heartbeat.

The wind came and blew soft wisps of air kisses on my cheeks, forehead and the top of my head. The sun caressed my body and warmed me clear through until I glowed in spirit light. I felt the Earth Mother pulling me into her arms cradling, rocking me. She showed me my place among all my brothers and sisters. I heard her heartbeat as she spoke. I felt the rhythms of the earth pulse me. I was one with her richness and I was nourished fully.

As I lay in her arms, feeling her strength pulse me, I breathed in the fragrances of flowers, grasses, herbs and trees. I saw herds of animals running free, mustangs, wolves, deer, antelope, buffalo, and sheep. I witnessed thousands of birds in flight, all sizes and colors, from the great hawks to tiny sparrows and hummingbirds. Then I experienced the great ocean. I experienced the mystery of the sea continually rolling and moving. I swam with the dolphins and whales. Their love enveloped me, opened me. I experienced the dessert sand and wildflowers in bloom and the dry breath of the air. I visited the mountain ranges and felt the power of the ancients' stories of the earth and the earth's movement under the surface of the solid ground, fluidity everywhere.

Then I was alone with the heartbeat of the Earth Mother and I was held firmly to her bosom.

One with the Universe

On my personal medicine path, I have experienced oneness and bliss. This is one of these experiences that helped me know I am never alone really, even though I find myself stuck in aloneness beliefs. When I step back and witness myself and my journey, I have plenty of evidence to the contrary.

I've just moved in with Anne, her daughter and another couple while I regroup and get my healing practice on solid ground. In every aspect, living here is a boost to strong healing. I am totally supported by all the house members. They see me as an asset to the household. They invited me to live with them not only to give me a place to live but also in the belief that my energy and skills would support them as well. They are glad to have me as part of their household. I arrange healing sessions as trade for my rent. With this as a foundation I move in.

One Sunday night, it is quite late, near midnight; Anne comes into my room to pull a Mayan Oracle card—I have her deck in my room. We're seated on my bed, and I decide to pull a card, too. As Anne reads my card to me, a strange feeling comes over me and I begin to breathe like the wind. As I breathe and listen to Anne, I say, "Oh, my God, this wind sound feels like an energy portal," and as I speak, I feel myself shoot out of my crown chakra into space. In this out-of-body journey, I seem to travel through space a great distance, traveling and traveling and traveling and traveling and traveling and traveling and traveling and traveling ….

After quite a while, I begin to feel like I was wrapped in a cocoon of light. In the cocoon, I was drawn to put my hands up over my head, and I felt myself spinning in a spiral upward. Then I shot out of the cocoon. I found myself lying face down with my arms spread out to either side, floating free in space. Then as I floated, I disintegrated; I merged fully with the Universe, like a raindrop into a pond. I became one with God and the Universe. After some time, I don't know how long, I experienced myself re-forming, integrating back into myself and as I did I felt myself coming back into my physical body where I was still sitting on the bed next to Anne.

I knew Anne had remained sitting on the bed; she had not traveled with me. At other times we have journeyed to together. Upon my return, I looked over at her and she said, "I saw your journey. I saw your amazing journey."

I said, "Well, what did you see?"

And she said, "It all started when you made your wind sound."

I love the wind sound.

"And then I saw you just shoot out of your body from your chest. I saw this energy just move out of your chest and go and go and go and go, I mean you were so far out there; you just went and went and went and went, you were traveling so far out. And then all of a sudden, I saw the dolphins and whales come and they started swimming around you in this circular motion, swimming in a figure eight motion all around you. They seemed to invite you to swim with them and you sort of stood up in the middle of their energy and put your hands over your head, and you swam with them for awhile, and then you shot out, like you had been shot from a cannon. Then you were lying with your arms outstretched, face down in the Universe. You totally disintegrated and were one with the Universe and God. After a while I saw you re-integrate, come back into your energetic self and just drop back down into your body and come back here."

I was thrilled by her witnessing. It validated my experience. I didn't know about the dolphins and the whales. That additional information touched me. In the months previous during my meditations, the dolphins and whales had appeared and worked with me. I felt their presence as I worked with clients also. Having them on this journey told me they were here to guide me. This was an added delight.

We talked for a long time about the feeling of oneness, this love state. It filled the whole room and us as we sat together, my friend and me.

PART FOUR

Healing Exercises

Introduction

The preverbal primal wound, the hole, the void—an adoptee feels this from the loss of their birthmother's heartbeat. When a child loses connection to their mother before words, it creates an underdeveloped limbic brain where the ability to trust resides. Because of this underdevelopment, a child is hyper vigilant and acts out of the flight or fright until they can bond with their new parent(s) and develop trust. In a normal birth experience a child has nine months within the womb for bonding and an additional nine months outside of the womb to complete that bonding before the child is ready to be independent.

If this wound is not mended in childhood; adult adoptees may still feel the void and do many things to fill it. Some adoptees use sex to get enough physical touch, some use mind-altering substances to dull their feelings of the big dark hole and missing pieces they sense, and most feel a loneliness they can't explain. Some adoptees adopt other families to help them feel safe and then test them to see if they will be there to support them when things are less than perfect. Other adoptees keep secrets from their adoptive family; afraid they will be abandoned from this family too. Most of these creations are unconscious and stem from unresolved wounds and misconceptions held in the body's cell memory. The body is sending messages to somehow fill the loss, the deep felt hole within.

All of these disturbances and felt losses can be healed. The healing section of this book has detailed exercises to address these losses.

For me the most profound healings occur with divine guidance. Spiritual guides come in many forms, such as higher self, angels, animal allies (totems), the grandmother and grandfather ancestors of the medicine wheel, and the sacred energy of the Medicine Wheel itself, along with gifted healers and spiritual teachers in everyday life. Throughout PULLING ON NEW GENES, I have given examples of some of these experiences.

This section will provide healing exercises you can do for yourself. I have brought together the most essential exercises needed to heal a variety of core wounds. The accumulation of these exercises will bring fullness to an empty feeling heart, and they provide tools to address separation anxiety and the deep fear of being alone. Other exercises will provide ways to grieve the loss of your birth mother, birth father and birth family history, as well as provide ways to build a new and rooted foundation for you.

Additional exercises will assist you in creating healthy boundaries so you can stay within yourself during intimate relationships. These are exercises to help you stop the neediness game when the younger parts get triggered, and they detail ways to be in touch and to listen to these parts for healing. You will find an exercise to find your inner heart wisdom voice and receive help from within.

Within these exercises you will discover how to truly hear yourself, you will learn how to honor and love yourself and others just as you and they are. These exercises will bring you into a new state of balance and wholeness where the emptiness can live in the past and you can live life from your fullness. From wholeness all is possible—including feeling in, as well as part of, family. May these basic techniques nourish you and provide stability and comfort along your spiral journey back to love, and during the hearts journey home to your essential self.

On Creating Sacred Space

I suggest you create special space for yourself, a safe space for healing. You may choose to create an altar or an other sanctuary space for healing.

You want to focus on what you wish to heal. You can begin by writing an intention list of your desires. While holding these healing intentions in your mind, begin to notice what objects or pictures will support these desires. You might find a picture of a healed person, or a symbol or picture of a spiritual master you feel connected with, like St. Francis, The Blessed Mother, Quan Yin, or Buddha—whomever you choose for your alter will be right for you.

When I create my altar I like to honor Mother Earth by placing a bowl of water; a white candle, which clears energy and represents the element of fire; and something of the earth, like fresh flowers or crystals, and pictures or sculptures of animal allies. Sometimes I draw a picture of where I am and where I would like to be and place them on my altar. Some people have a permanent sacred place or altar and simply add items to match their healing intentions. I prefer to create a special space each time, because as I create the altar, I draw more and more clarity to myself for the actual healing. The ritual of creating an altar provides support for your process.

Altars may include a variety of items—a white candle to burn away whatever you wish to clear during your session; or minerals like rose quartz, amethyst, quartz crystal, turquoise or other minerals that promote healing and add support energy during your process. Some people use sage, evergreen or cedar to prepare their space and themselves, and while they smug, they ask to clear away earthly demands and confusion, thereby allowing them to go inside and listen and connect to their deeper wisdom within. Some people choose to use holy water or wear a gold cross during their healing process. Others place a glass bowl of blessed salt water on their altar to assist in keeping their space clear of unwanted energy. All of these methods or any combination of methods and items can help to create sacred space and ready you for your healing process. You may wish to play classical or soothing meditation music in the background while you do your healing—I prefer silence or my drum and rattles.

If altars and rituals are not your thing, just find a place where you can do the following exercises in quiet without interruption, where you feel safe. Turn off your phone and find a comfortable place to sit. Begin the healing process from there.

Once you've created your space, sit quietly without being disturbed for an hour or so. Get comfortable; sit rather than lie down because you will be more affective and be less inclined to fall asleep; then close your eyes and take a few deep breaths, and quiet yourself.

Note: I recommend that you read these exercises into a tape player, so you can simply close your eyes and listen and be in the healing process. Meditations Exercises 1, 2, and 3 can be done as one long meditation or as three short experiences. All other exercises stand alone.

Exercise 1: Guided Meditation for Creating Sacred Space

Get comfortable, close your eyes, take a deep breath in and let it go. Again in, breathing in peacefulness and bringing out tension, breathing in joy, breathing out frustration, breathing in fresh air, breathing out staleness … and begin to imagine you are sitting in a beautiful pyramid of golden light … And the light within this pyramid totally surrounds your body… Take another deep breath in and let it go… Imagine too that there is a mirror image of this pyramid beneath you grounding you into the earth … creating a structure of light all around you … Breath in the light, feel its warmth and relax …

Exercise 2: Guided Meditation for Opening your Chakras (internal energy centers)

Now imagine there is a ball of light in the top of the pyramid and begin to bring this golden ball of light down through the top of your head through your crown area … opening the crown charka in the top of your head … allow the light to filter down through the crown into the center of your head and expand it out so that all the cells in your head become one with the light, relaxed yet alert now … take another breath in, and as you exhale … relax and let all the tension of the day drift away … becoming more and more relaxed with each breath you take… Now imagine the light moving in and out of the center of your forehead, opening up this energy center to the light … and as you imagine this, feel this energy coming in and out of this area in the center of your forehead, opening this energy center for new awareness and clarity for you… And know as you sit in sacred space and work with this guided meditation this process will get easier and easier for you … Over time you will develop new ways of sensing, feeling or seeing the light energy, so for now… relax and allow this golden light to move from your head now down to your throat … and allow the light to massage your throat, opening up the throat to the light… Readying your throat to speak your truth… When you feel each center opening, simply move to the next…. breathing in and out and … and imagine the light moving from the throat now down to the heart … bringing warmth and a golden glow to the heart center…. Open your heart to this warmth by imagining your heart as a flower unfolding – opening to the warmth of the sun and your breath …. Stay here in the heart feeling yourself nurtured by the light… and notice the rhythm of your heartbeat … your rhythm your vibration … and breathe … And now, allow yourself to go deeper within the heart … ask to go to your deeper heart, your soul heart, your wisdom heart…. we all know this place… ask to go to this place and sit there with yourself ….

…. Good … and when you're ready … bring the golden light from the heart center to the upper belly and open up the solar plexus charka to the light…. Sit there for awhile … feeling this energy center open…. And when you are ready …move on …. And bring the light to the lower belly … opening this energy center… and sit there for a while … now bring the light from the lower belly to the base of your spine your root charka … opening this energy center to the light and once you feel your connection at the base of your spine, imagine a cord of light running from the base of your spine into the center of the earth grounding you in the earth. … Great, and know now that you are connected to heaven and earth and yourself for all your knowing.

Note: This meditation is a powerful way to connect before each healing process. It opens and connects you to yourself and the Divine and the Earth and provides an inner connectedness that supports inner listening.

You may choose at this point to invite in your spiritual guides or guardians, or you may choose to do this before you enter into the guided meditation.

Exercise 3: Guided Meditation for Calling Guides and Spirit Helpers:

Speak: "Guardians from the light, please come and be with me and assist me on my healing journey." You may choose to know them and can say, "Show yourselves to me. Let me know your presence."

Sometimes a friend or loved one who has passed away will come, sometimes an old pet will appear; sometimes you may feel a touch on your shoulder or a loving presence. Trust these moments. You can always ask, "Who is with me from the light?" If you feel a strange presence that makes you uncomfortable, you can ask who it is or simply ask the energy to go to the light and leave your space now.

If you are unaware of guides or elders who work with you, there are some exercises to introduce you to your helpers later. Angels and your Higher Self must be called; they are always present but to work with you they must be invited. I call them like this; "Angels, Arch Angels, please come and be with me now; I would like your presence with me for this healing. Higher Self, please work with me now." I call all my guides and animal allies as well whenever I create my sacred space and as they come I thank them by saying, "thank you for coming, I am grateful for your presence." Be aware at the end of each meditation your feelings of gratitude and acknowledge your helpers and yourself.

Now you are ready to listen to yourself and ask questions or proceed with a healing exercise.

Note abuse survivors: If opening you charka centers or connecting to different parts of your body causes fear or anxiety, skip the chakra-opening segment. You can simply see yourself within the pyramid of light or within a column of light and breathe in this light, allowing it to fill your heart. Then if you choose, you can allow the light to fill you entire body, bringing you into a warm cocoon of protective light from the outside and from within. This can be your beginning place to begin a healing exercise.

Exercise 4: Guided Meditation for Connecting to your Higher Self

Get comfortable, close your eyes, and take a nice deep breath in and let it go, letting go of all distractions around you … Bring your attention to your breath, breathing in and out. Begin to notice where your body touches the chair … and allow your entire body to be supported by the chair… Relaxing deeply into the support of the chair… Take another deep breath in and let it go … allowing you to go deeper and deeper into relaxation and calm… Now imagine if you will that you find yourself on a sandy path, walking … walking through an expansive meadow, the sun is shining brightly and you can feel the sun's warmth on your body. It kisses your face and cheeks with a warm soft breeze. The sky is bright and deep blue … and you notice while you walk there are animals at play … And a profuse array of wild flowers in bloom … providing color candy for your eyes and a generous bouquet of scents for your senses.

You are on your way to find your Higher Self and dive deeper into the mystery of yourself. As you make your way down the path … you notice out in the distance, there is a stand of ancient oak trees and you begin to head in this direction, somehow knowing this will be a good meeting place to find your Higher Self… and as you arrive at the oak trees … there sitting under a the largest tree, is your Higher Self… She/he beckons you to come and sit down and rest awhile. You sit and face your Higher Self feeling the energy between you …. And you begin to get acquainted… you ask as many questions as you wish… And you listen for you Higher Self's response. You may choose to ask, for instance, what is your name, what is your purpose, will you guide me, how do I contact you, and how do I stay connected with you? And you listen and remember everything you have heard.

Now, look closely at your Higher Self and notice, and feel into this experience. Breathe in and take this new knowing into your body, mind and spirit… and spend as much time as you need … being with your Higher Self.

And when you feel complete … begin to notice where you are sitting in the chair … and very slowly wiggle your hands and feet and bring you consciousness back to where you are sitting, bringing with you the full experience of meeting your Higher Self, and very gently come back to the room, noticing where you are sitting, coming back to full awareness feeling, alive, alert and fully present.

Exercise 5: Guided Meditation for Connecting to Spirit

Get comfortable, close your eyes, breathe in and out and let the day go … go into that quiet place inside and breathe… Feel all the places your body touches the chair and let the chair totally support your body… breathe … close your eyes and imagine you are surrounded by a beautiful column of golden light, feel the warmth of the light surround your body as your body becomes more and more relaxed, limp and heavy in your chair … with the knowing that all is well in your sacred space … breath in and relax even deeper now…notice your face, eyes, noise and mouth totally one with the light and relaxed … your scalp, forehead, cheeks and jaw, one with the light and totally relaxed, your neck and throat, one with the light, relaxed… imagine if you would that there are tiny fingers of light massaging you shoulders and neck area and any tension that is there is gone… let the fingers move all the way down your spine now … releasing any tension there … bringing in the light… your chest, back, belly and arms now totally relaxed …one with the light, finger tip and hands relaxed … seat, legs, ankles and feet relaxed, all the way to the tip of your toes, relaxed one with the light. Imagine too that there is a grounding cord of light running from the base of your tailbone into the earth…one with the light, heaven and earth.

And from this connected … relaxed space I want you to become aware now of Spirit just for you. Let spirit be with you … show itself to you… be with the feeling of spirit … just for you … … … … … … … … … … … … … … Pause here as long as you need to connect with spirit just for you…

When you feel complete, very gently begin to notice where you are sitting in the chair, notice your feet on the floor and begin to come back into the room fully present, alive awake and renewed ready for your day bringing with you … your experience of spirit just for you.

You may wish to draw a picture of spirit or write your experience. It is helpful during each exercise to capture the essence of your experience in some way; it grounds the experience into your consciousness for future reference.

Exercise 6: Inner Children Dialogue

This exercise explores ways to listen, heal, and connect with your inner children—and to find the ones who are lost, lonely, scared, hurt, angry and separate.

There are certain things to consider while working with your inner children; **you must be sensitive with all these younger parts** of yourself. For the most part, when we feel triggered, it is a part of our self that feels threatened, and this part is simply acting out, acting out of fear from an earlier situation stored in our body memory. When we are young and don't know how to deal with a particular situation, we store this information, this story, in our cells. Later when we have more adult resources, these unfinished dilemmas surface so that we can resolve and heal them. We get triggered and overreact because we are responding as a younger one, which is disconnected from our adult wisdom. We are out of alignment within ourselves. The disassociated part, acts out to gain control and feel safe.

When we act inappropriately, feel ashamed, and wrong our self, we try to get rid of our behavior. In doing this, we essentially push the younger parts away, abandoning our younger ones' feelings. I am not saying that acting out is the right thing to do, but I am saying when we act out, we need to discover why we got triggered and heal, come into alignment and balance with our self. One way to accomplish this is, after an incident, to find this part of the self that is scared, hurt, and lonely, the one who acted out, and deeply listen. Take responsibility to notice you're upset without making yourself feel wrong for it. Write down what occurred so you can set aside time later, when you have some distance, to dialogue with yourself. It is important to realize that these inner children are part of us, and by not honoring them and working with them, we remain out of balance and continue to bring the cycle of upset into our life.

It is important to find out what will allow the younger parts of our self to feel safe, secure and loved. When we can meet our younger ones needs—give them what they need, then we are on the way to balance, healing, and inner peace. After you have completed a healing session with yourself, then you can go back to the person or situation where you over-reacted and have a clearing, apologize and move on.

If you try these exercises and you surface terror, or find it too frightening to continue, your inner children are letting you know that you need a skilled person to work with. I suggest that you find an early childhood development therapist, a hypnotherapist or a shaman to help. Someone that understands early childhood development can work with you in a loving, safe way to uncover and heal the younger ones traumas someone that can help you build a new foundation; preferably, a therapist who has experience working with adoptees and their special needs.

Healing the little one(s) who are upset:

Begin by writing out an incident you wish to heal. Be specific. Then sit quietly within sacred space, connecting to yourself and your spirit guides. Before you begin to work, ask your guides and guardians to be with you and to support you on your healing journey. Know that you are in touch with the spirit, your higher self and your heart. Once you feel these connections, then you can begin to listen and ask: who got upset, or what got triggered, by the incident you have written down. Listen closely and dialogue with the one who is upset.

You may ask:

Why are you upset? How old are you? What do you want? When and where did you learn this? Who told you this? Do you live inside or outside of the body? Where are you in the body?

The Dialogue may go like this:

"I'm thee."

My reply:"Hi, three-year-old, thanks for showing yourself to me and talking with me, I'm really glad to meet you. Tell me, where are you in my body?"

"I'm here in the belly (or the left arm or shoulder, or…)."

Focus where they say they are—and remember, sometimes you may feel two or three places within the body that is triggered by an incident. Usually this means there is more than one split-out part you need to talk with. Ask again, "Why are you upset?"

"I'm all alone, I'm so scared."

Keep talking until you find a way to comfort this part of you. "Tell me more."

"I'm afraid I'll never be good enough for Mom, and she'll leave too. I try to be good but sometimes I get mad and yell. I'm so afraid she'll leave me, my first Mom did."

Reassure this one that you are with them and you won't leave them. Let this younger part know you will be with them no matter what. They might point out—you did leave them, that you pay no attention to them when they get mad. Tell them you will set up a time to talk with them so they can begin to trust you, and do this.

I might say, "I'm here, I will always be here for you now. I didn't know what to do before, but now I do, I'm glad I found you now, I am here."

Know if you think of something later you forgot to say, you can always talk to this part of yourself and tell them more, just remember **to listen to their reply.**

Next, I might ask, "Would you like to crawl into my arms so I can hold you?" You can hold a stuffed animal in your arms and imagine this animal is this younger part of you, and talk to this one until they feels safe and calm: "I want you to know, young one, that our mom loves us no matter what, even when we are upset or she is upset, she still loves us, she won't leave us … Do you understand?"

She might not have a response.

I ask, "How did you get in the belly, what happened, why did you go there?"

She might say, "Mom was really mad at me for … I went to the belly to hide."

Next I would introduce her to the heart, telling her that the heart beats 24 hours a day, and it sends out love with each and every beat. I'd ask, "Would you like to come back up to the heart where you can feel love with every heart beat?" If this is okay, I'll say, "Come on up to my heart, I'll lead you with my hand into the heart. Follow my hand up into the heart."

Some people visualize energy or a young baby moving from their belly up to the heart. They see this young one safely in the heart, content, warm and safe. The baby falls to sleep safe and at peace. They feel free from anxiety. They are free from fear. Others sense the younger one crawling to the heart; sometimes it feels as if they simply jump in, but always when they come home to the heart, they feel love and safety there.

When you feel the young one home in the heart, welcome them. "Welcome home, little one, welcome home to the heart. Can you feel the heart beat? … I want you to know with every beat of the heart you are loved unconditionally, just the way you are, 24 hours a day, no matter what. Welcome home to the heart, welcome home to me. Thank you for being so brave and talking to me today. I am so glad you are home."

Sometimes inner children need attention before they are willing to come home to the heart. It is important to set up regular meeting times to dialogue with these younger parts until they are ready to transition to the heart. Some young ones need extra attention and reassurance even after they have come into the heart. I like to introduce them to my guardian angels and higher self so they can feel hugged and nurtured all the time. I then dialogue with them until they feel secure.

You can also dialogue with them by drawing a picture of an inner child, and then listen inside and dialogue with the picture you have drawn. Once, I drew four of my inner children and had a daily conversation with them for the months.

I wrote out these conversations, at the base of each picture—my questions their answers, their questions, my answers, until we had nothing more to say. This conversation satisfied the needs of each one being heard and seen. One day there was no more dialogue, they were all happy and content and complete within themselves and within me. I felt integrated in some way, more energized and whole.

The key is to this dialogue is to enjoy and learn from each found part of you. There is always a gift. When you discover the gift you have healed the incident, the trigger and the inner child. Remember we are always evolving, so even though we heal one area and gain strength and balance, there is always an opportunity to go deeper, surface another area within our self. If we face things as they arise, life becomes easier and less complicated. As we complete with our past stories, we have no need to recreate similar stories to interact with, we are complete, and we have come into balance.

Terms:

Abandonment: feeling like someone is always going to leave

Hurt: someone close doesn't hear you, or someone else gets the attention you feel you should have gotten

Anger: Having a tantrum over something trivial—like the cleaners pressed your slacks wrong

With these feelings you can do self-healing by asking where are these feeling coming from; who inside is holding this belief, or is mad, scared you are leaving, or feeling hurt; when did these feelings begin; how old were you?

Just ask: the first time I felt this feeling, how old was I? Then ask to talk with yourself at that age. Comfort yourself and give yourself what you missed or what is needed. Usually listening to your story and being acknowledged and heard is what you need, or being held if you are scared and alone. You can call on your higher self, the angels, and animal totems to energetically hold you.

Exercise 7: Mirrors

Noticing how others respond to us can help us see what is going on inside us. When we can determine what is happening within, we can begin to take responsibility for our own actions. Instead of blaming other people for their actions, we learn to see what we are doing that may cause others to react to us.

The list below is a sample of items to aid self-awareness:
If you judge and criticize yourself, others will judge and criticize you.
If you hurt yourself, others will hurt you.
If you lie to yourself, other will lie to you.
If you are irresponsible to yourself, others will be irresponsible in relationship to you.
If you blame yourself, others will blame you.
If you do violence to yourself emotionally, others will do violence to you emo tionally, or even physically.
If you don't listen to your feelings, no one will listen to your feelings.
If you love yourself, others will love you.
If you respect yourself, others will respect you.
If you trust yourself, others will trust you.
If you are honest with yourself, others will be honest with you.
If you are gentle and compassionate with yourself, others will treat you with compassion.
If you appreciate yourself, others with appreciate you.
If you honor yourself, others will honor you.
If you enjoy yourself, others will enjoy you.

I felt at times I was not honored and blamed people for not honoring my work. In fact what was occurring was that I was judging my work and not totally honoring my creations and myself. When I began to honor my work, my clients began to honor my work and me in new ways. They referred me to new clients and thanked me for my work regularly.

Exercise 8: Guided Meditation for Discovering the Male and Female Within

Have a pen and pad nearby. Get comfortable, close your eyes, take a few deep breaths, breathing in love, breathing out tension, breathing in quiet, breathing out frustration, breathing in calm, breathing out frustration, and begin to feel yourself relaxing from the top of your head all the way down your body to the tips of your toes.

Close your eyes and allow yourself to just be with your process. Now take a moment and imagine a man whom you truly love and admire. When you have a clear image of this person—it can be a famous person or someone you know or someone from history— when you have this image … begin to notice what are the specific qualities and characteristic of this person whom you love and admire. When you feel you have gleaned all these qualities: write these down.

When you have finished writing … put your pen and pad away, close your eyes and take another deep breath in and out … letting the image of this man go… on your next intake of breath, bring into your conscious a woman whom you truly love and admire. When she is fully present in your mind … notice what are the qualities and characteristics of this woman whom you love and admire. When she is totally present with you: Write the qualities and characteristics that you admire and love down on your pad. Breathe and bring yourself back to a present state by noticing where you are sitting and your feet resting on the floor.

Look at these qualities and characteristics. Circle any that are not you. You will find that most of the qualities you listed are within you. If you love and admire these qualities, then they are within you—maybe not fully developed, but all these qualities and characteristics mirror different aspects of you. If they were not part of you, then you couldn't see them in others. Now, take ten minutes sit quietly or journal and take in your fullness.

Exercise 9: Art Exercises for Getting to know Mother Earth and Yourself

Begin to notice the weather the wind, rain, sun, and snow. Notice the rhythm of the moons, align yourself with the season that you are experiencing right now—when it is raining, cleanse and replenish yourself; when the snow falls and quiets the earth, go inside to your own inner quiet; when the sunshine peeks through your window on an early morning visit, arise and greet the sun with gratitude and delight. Learn to move through the day with the flavor of each day, noticing the changes, the beauty, the smells, tastes and delights of each day. Let the earth awaken you to all your senses.

Draw, paint or color from this awakened state any aspect of nature you choose. Begin to realize that you to are part of this magnificence, you are related to the Great Mother and all who walk this earth walk—animals, minerals, plants and people alike. Enjoy your day.

Discover treasures abundant in nature. Gather some fall leaves and paint them or mix them as a collage into an abstract painting. Make a table centerpiece with the multi-colored leaves. Visit a tree for an hour or an afternoon and notice its presence, its shades of color, texture and size. Notice yourself in relationship with the tree. Pick up a deer antler and use it as a handle for a basket or a rattle. Discover smooth warn sticks from a lake's edge, and use this stick to create a prayer stick or walking stick, decorating it with symbols that reflect your personal or spiritual journey. You may choose to decorate your stick with leather wrapping, found feathers, representations of where you have been and where you're headed and what you want to bring into your life now. You may choose to decorate it simple for beauty's sake, then each time you see your treasure, you will be reminded that beauty is all around you and is you too. You might bring home seaweed and shells and place them on a shelf to remind you of the sea. Simply notice the ebb and flow and drop in with it. Take a walk in the forest or along a beach and the let your senses lead you. Walk in all kinds of weather and expand your senses.

Make a collage of the Earth Mother and tell a friend about the collage when you are finished. Let all you say enter you, and feel your connection to the Earth and the Universe and all its wisdom. Begin to feel these connections.

Make a collage of the mother you always wanted. Discover what is missing in your life and give yourself the experiences that will fill these voids in your life.

Draw an animal you are particularly connected with or find a picture of this animal and sit and meditate with this animal—see how you are similar to this animal. Notice the strengths and qualities of this animal and see where you might want to expand yourself. You may choose to use this animal as your guide.

Draw who you are today and simply be present to yourself.

Exercise 10: Guiding Meditation for Becoming one with Mother Earth

Get comfortable, close your eyes, and take a few deep breaths in and on… the out breath let go of your day and your surroundings… breath in and notice all the places your body touches the chair and allow the chair to fully support your body, relax into the chair. Now imagine that you are in a favorite spot in nature, it could be on a sandy beach with the sound of ocean waves lapping the shore, or a beautiful meadow full of wild flowers and tall grasses with animals scampering about, you might choose a mountain top covered in soft dry snow … wherever you choose to be… Simply be there and take time to look around and notice what is in your world… in your favorite place in nature. Notice the color of the sky, the air on your face, the scents all around you… listen to the sounds all around you, are there birds singing, animals running, what is present in your landscape… how far you can see, what does it feel like to be here? Now find a spot where you can sit or lay down and rest yourself in this beautiful place.

You might find you are sitting at a base of a large tree and if you are … allow yourself to nestle in deeper feeling the bark as it supports your back, and merge deeper until you can feel the energy of the tree, the sap running inside its trunk, and the quiet magnitude of the tree … you may want to spread your arms open wide and reach for the sky and sun the way the tree does … And feel your feet rooted deeply into the earth gathering nourishment from the soil.… Let the tree show you its strength and flexibility. You and the tree are one. Feel the sun on your leaves, and the wind as it whispers through your branches … be the tree … look at all the colors of green, and shades of brown you are … what insects eat you… who is playing or nesting in your branches … how many creatures do you support … connect to the roots and feel into how deep they go into the earth … feel the ground beneath you … feel your roots … you and the tree are one. Breathe.

You may find yourself lying next to a rushing river, allow yourself to become one with the river's flow, let it pulse you and begin to carry you downstream, you and the river are one, you ripple over rocks warn smooth by your touch, you move into the deep bottom and slow becoming quiet and lazy until the next bend where you pick up your speed and form rapids again. You and the river are one, moving in the flow of life … moving with great speed and meandering along. Allow yourself to become one with a rock and feel the river caressing your surface as it moves and washes you clean. The river and the rock and you are one.

Maybe you find yourself standing next to a waterfall, crashing to the earth. Jump in stand in the power of the water as it rushes over you, let the water cleanse you and then become one with the waterfall, feel the space between where you can breath easy, feel the force and strength pulse you notice where you land on the earth pool and the quietness below your force … be the sparkle that catches the sun or the drop that smoothed out the rock, be the drop who becomes one with the pool below … you and the waterfall are one, you and the water are one.

Maybe you find yourself lying on the ground, on the great earth mother, she is all around you supporting your entire life… as you lie there you begin to notice her soils temperature, dry or wet? You begin to breathe in the earth beneath you and as you do you become one with the soil, its depth and its texture you feel it within yourself, the earth is wrapping you in a beautiful cocoon … which totally and completely nurtures and feeds every cell of your body … you are one with the earth and all your needs are met … you are cradled in the womb of the great mother… you drink in her fragrances and are nurtured at her breast, she holds you in unconditional love, and protects you in her womb and in this safe space of love and comfort … she shows you all you need to see… all her creatures and where you fit… she speaks to your soul of all that is… You are one with the Earth Mother… she and you are one.

When you feel complete, begin to notice where you are sitting and very gently wiggle your fingers and toes and begin to come back into the room fully present, noticing your surroundings, feeling refreshed, renewed and ready for your day.

Draw or make notes of your experience if you wish. It is always nice to have a reminder of your experience for the times you feel alone or lost, and then you can re-visit this place and know you are one with the earth and the universe.

Exercise 11: Connecting and Replenishing the Heart Wounds—Three guided meditations.

As adoptees we lost the sound of our Mother's heartbeat. These three experiences assist in replenishing the heart.

A. Guided Meditation to Connect to the Birth-Mother's Heartbeat

Get comfortable, close your eyes, and take a nice deep breath in and let it go … Feel yourself relaxing … let the tension in your body go … notice all the places your body touches the chair and let your body totally be supported by the chair. Relax and breath … we are going to take a journey back in time to when you were still in the womb and connected to your mother's heart beat … but before we go on this journey we need to create safety for you. Who do you want to go on this journey with you? Call them in now … call your guides and animal allies to be with you now … call your Higher Self to watch over this journey … When you sense, see or feel these helpers with you … breathe and relax and know with every breath you take and each word you hear … you will go deeper and deeper into relaxation and calm.

Imagine and feel the golden light all around you … Breathe … Feel all the tension in your body release … become limp, loose and comfortable. Breathe … From the top of your head to the base of your spine … relaxed, comfortable … imagine a golden cord of light from the base of your spine running into the earth, grounding you now … Breathe… Your arms and legs relaxed, to the tips of your fingers and toes. All tension gone … relaxed …

Now imagine that you can simply float back in time … to the time of this life when you are an infant in the womb of your mother. You are in the safety of this womb and all is well. You are moving and one with the heart beat of your mother. All is well. Feel this heart beat and fill your heart until you feel full.

Remember this heart and the warmth and nurturing of this heart … knowing this time you will be able to bring this knowing this fullness back with you into your adult life. You will be able to know this fullness from this day forward. You can feel this heartbeat now … it beats within you and your heart. … feel it … sense it … let your heart open to this heartbeat now… great! Breathe …. Sit with this fullness …

know you will bring this fullness back with you into current time, but for now ….
Breathe…..

When you feel complete and can feel the heartbeat of your mother, I want you
to begin to come back to present time, bringing with you the beat of your mother's
heart, bringing with you the fullness you feel in your heart, and very slowly I'd like
to you notice where you are sitting on your chair … notice your hands and feet and
wiggle your fingers and toes and very gently begin to come back, back to the sacred
space where you began with this fullness and the beat of your mother's heart. Very
gently opening your eyes coming back, refreshed, renewed, fully back, knowing this
love.

B. Connecting to the Heartbeat of Mother Earth

Get comfortable and relax, close your eyes, take a nice deep breath in and let
it go, relax … Notice all the places your body touches your chair and let the chair
totally support your body … close your eyes … let go … breathe and relax … Today
we are going to take a journey where we will be held and loved by Great Mother
Earth, and during this journey you will have the opportunity to connect with her
heartbeat and her love. So breathe in and as you exhale … simply release your day
… letting go into comfort … loose, limp, relaxed.

Imagine if you would you are in your favorite place in nature. You are there.
You can see, smell, taste, hear and sense this place and all that is around you. Begin
to notice, look all around, and take in all you see—the colors of the sky and earth.
Is anyone with you, are there animals about? Just notice and take in what you see,
smell the air and sense all the creatures, big and small, that are with you in this
beautiful natural place in nature. Notice the colors of the trees, of the ground cover;
smell their aromas as they are released into the air. What minerals are there? Notice
them. Are there clouds in the sky, or is it clear, what colors do you see or imagine…
Listen to the sweet sounds around you, is there a stream or an ocean, are you in the
desert or the mountains? Notice …. Notice the creatures large and small around
you… and take in all this beauty and notice everything… Breathe …

Now imagine yourself laying on the ground …the earth beneath totally supporting you… and begin to feel the pulse of the earth beneath you, let it beat
against and within you … this is the heart of the Mother … breathe in and let the
earth breathe you in … breathe out and feel the earth support you … the ground
below you supports you … and the sky above and the air all around supports you…
breathe with the rhythm of the earth and notice how you and the earth are one …

breathe … and allow the Earth Mother to show you anything she wishes … let her hold you in her belly … let her rock you, let her breathe life into you … breathe in and let this fullness in … Become one with the Mother's pulse, her heartbeat, and one with yourself… Breathe … Know the earth is always breathing with you … she is always beneath your feet … she is always supporting and feeding you… You and the Earth Mother are one … thank her for showing you her ways … breathe her in and when you feel complete … begin to notice where you are sitting, wiggle your fingers and toes and begin to come back into the present with the knowing that you and the Earth Mother are one, you and all the creatures are related, she is always here with you whenever you need her … and when you are ready … very gently begin to come back by noticing where you are sitting, begin to bring your awareness back to your body, coming back to present time … renewed, refreshed and ready for your day.

C. Connecting to the Soul Heart the Divine Wisdom of the Heart

Within your sacred space, get comfortable, close your eyes and take a nice deep breath in and let it go, and enter inner quiet of you… and begin to notice all the places your body touches the chair and let your body be totally supported by the chair … relax and breathe … and imagine if you will that you are sitting in a beautiful column of golden light … and this column expands in both directions to connect you to heaven and earth … see and sense yourself in this column of light … great… now imagine that above your head is a golden ball of light … see up there and begin to bring this light in through the top of your head, down into the center of your head, and allow the light to expand out and touch every cell in your head … and as it does, your head becomes relaxed …. And breathe … let the light come in and out of your third eye …that area in the middle of your forehead … breathe … now move the light down to your throat … opening that energy center to the light … great … once you can feel the warmth of the light in the throat … focus your attention on your heart … and bring the golden light there … and once you reach your heart … breathe … feeling the divine golden light entering your heart … opening your heart to the light … imagine too that there is a cranberry colored inner tube of light surrounding your entire chest and back area … providing you with extra love protection around your heart center, feel this protection and breathe … now bring your attention back to your heart and allow it to open like a lotus flower … open to you and go to the core at the center of your heart … knowing that you already know this place … just go there… and find the flame that is you … your core loving self … your divine heart … your wisdom heart … and just be here with yourself and your soul … listen … sense … be … be present with yourself … enjoy the love the bliss and the knowing … welcome home.

When you feel full and complete … know you will from this day forward know this place … you can return to it anytime you wish … after a while, you will discover you are this place … but for now … begin to notice where you are sitting on the chair, wiggle your fingers and your toes and very gently begin to come back into the room by opening your eyes and coming back.

Exercise 12: Guiding Meditation for Connecting the Divine Heart Energy with the Limbic Brain

Being separated from our mother's heartbeat stimulated our reptilian brain to develop a vigilant protective watch over us to secure our safety. Whenever we feel threatened, therefore, we go into "fright and flight" response. Connecting our heart to the limbic brain opens and strengths both these centers so we are triggered less and can experience more fullness.

The Meditation:

The limbic brain resides in the center of your head. If you ask to become aware of this area, you will go there.

When you feel you have located this center brain area, imagine it filled with golden light. Great! Now move your focus to your center heart, your wise and divine heart, and connect there. When you can feel this connection … imagine … sense the light in your heart … the divine present … and with this heart connection … imagine a golden cord of light connecting your heart center with the your center brain … the limbic brain … and breathe in and out, feeling this connection. Imagine this connection getting stronger and stronger until you know this connection is stable … then when you feel it is complete … you may feel as if there is one voice, one tone, from this area now … then you can begin to bring your focus back to the room … feeling refreshed and renewed and more solid in yourself.

Exercise 13: Using full body awareness in making decisions

Write out a question you have:

     With your question firmly in your mind, close your eyes and get quiet. Breathe, relaxing your body but keeping your question in mind. Focus your attention on the third eye area in your head and ask for guidance on your question from this focus point. When you have an answer, open your eyes and write it down.

Third Eye Answer:

     Now move your focus to your heart and, with your question in mind, ask for an answer from your heart center. Listen and when you get an answer, open your eyes and write it down.

Heart Center Answer:

     Continue the same process and focus your attention on your upper belly, the solar plexus area. Close your eyes and ask your question; when you get an answer write it down.

Solar Plexus (belly)—Center Answer:

When you have gotten answers from these three areas, close your eyes and ask for an integrated answer; when you have received this answer, write it down.

Whole Body Integration Answer:

Summary: After Healing

With each healing comes a gift of new awareness—to enjoy the gifts along your life journey. When you can see the gifts from an old wound, you have healed that wound. Begin to notice, as you heal yourself, everything outside yourself is different in your relationships and in how you connect to your friends and your environment. Celebrate your healings; this is essential in this process because it acknowledges your progress and empowers the self to handle whatever comes up next.

Healing is an ongoing process. As we grow and change we spiral to a new level of understanding. We come more into our deeper knowing and can begin to come into inner peacefulness. With each new experience our wounds may be triggered, but now there is a way to recognize where you are on the spiral of change—and to choose how you want to change and heal.

Enjoy your journey with blessing and love.

—Liz

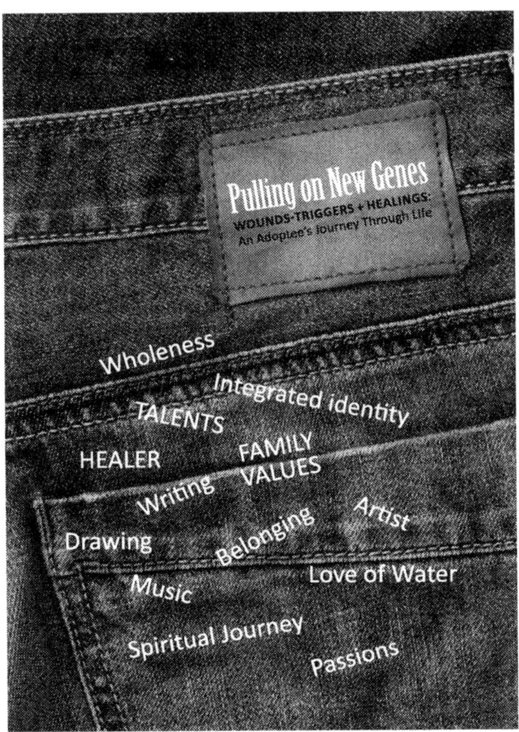